Scottish Mountaineering Club

District Guide Books

MUNRO'S TABLES

General Editor: MALCOLM SLESSER

Five Sisters of Kintail from Mam Ratagan.

SCOTTISH MOUNTAINEERING CLUB

DISTRICT GUIDE BOOKS

Munro's Tables

OF THE 3000-FEET
MOUNTAINS OF SCOTLAND

AND OTHER TABLES
OF LESSER HEIGHTS

Revised by J. C. Donaldson and W. L. Coats

THE SCOTTISH MOUNTAINEERING TRUST

EDINBURGH

First published in Great Britain in 1969 by
THE SCOTTISH MOUNTAINEERING TRUST
369 High Street, Edinburgh, 1

Copyright © 1969 by The Scottish Mountaineering Trust

First published 1891
Revised and republished 1921
Enlarged and republished 1933
New edition 1953
1953 Edition revised 1969
Reprinting history excluded

Designed for the Scottish Mountaineering Trust by
West Col Productions

WHOLESALE DISTRIBUTORS
West Col Productions
1 Meadow Close
Goring   Reading RG8 OAP
Berks England

Set in Monotype Imprint Series 101 and Grotesque 215
Printed in England by Cox & Wyman Ltd, London, Reading and Fakenham

CONTENTS

ILLUSTRATIONS

FOREWORD

MUNRO'S TABLES are re-presented to the public simply through the enormous demand that exists for them. This volume represents the material contained in the 1953 edition brought up to date in certain aspects by Mr J. C. Donaldson and Mr W. L. Coats, to whom the S.M.C. Guide Book committee is much indebted.

The columns giving the map sheet numbers have been revised to fit in with the Seventh Series of the Ordnance Survey, and four figure map references have been added to the position columns.

Due, however, to pressure of time, both in revising and publishing this edition, heights have not been amended in accordance with some of the latest figures issued by the Ordnance Survey. Eventual conversion to the metric system will probably obviate complete up-dating in this respect.

No revision has been made of the " best ascended " column, and it should be borne in mind that the construction of dams or other features may have taken away or introduced essential features of the originally suggested routes.

MALCOLM SLESSER
Glasgow, *January* 1969

View west from Cairngorm to Cairn Toul and Braeriach

1

Munro's Tables

ALL THE SCOTTISH MOUNTAINS
3000 FEET IN HEIGHT AND ABOVE

Revised by the Compiler, the late
Sir HUGH T. MUNRO, Bart., of Lindertis
and rearranged by
Mr J. Gall Inglis, F.R.S.E.

PREFATORY NOTE to 1921 Edition

I⊤ is much to be regretted that Sir Hugh Munro did not live to carry through the press this revised edition of his Tables, for which he had been collecting material for many years. As he always welcomed information on the subject, and had himself visited all the 3000-feet tops in Scotland except one or two, his knowledge of them was probably second to none.

Unfortunately, his revision was only partially completed at the time of his death, and no definite information has been found as to his views on many facts that had been brought to his notice. In these circumstances, it has been thought desirable simply to reissue the Tables substantially as he left them, leaving the debatable questions of inserting additional tops, or of deleting old ones, to be settled when more complete information is available.

The main revision of the Tables was carried out by the late Mr J. R. Young, in consultation with various members of the S.M.C., from—

(a) A card index left by Sir Hugh Munro, on which he had recorded changes in classification, new tops, cancelled tops, and other notes.

(b) A list—prepared for Sir Hugh by Mr A. W. Peacock—of the many alterations made in the O.S. maps subsequently to the first publication of the Tables. The latest available maps were the Revised six-inch Survey of about 1897 onwards, and the Second Revision of the one-inch Survey, of about 1904–1907. The nature of these changes will be found on page 22.

The re-classifications of the new tops, cancelled tops, and separate mountains are all from Sir Hugh's card index, with only a few exceptions; but the sequence of the individual tops has been considerably modified by the replacement of many " contour " heights by " approx." heights, gleaned from the *S.M.C. Journal*, the hill-shaded 1-inch O.S. maps, and other sources mentioned in the footnotes, by Mr J. G. Inglis. He has also rearranged the individual tops under their respective " separate mountains", has prepared an alphabetical index, and has revised the " Position " and " Best Ascended From " columns.

The Scottish Mountaineering Club take this opportunity of thanking Sir Hugh Munro's executors for handing over to the Club for publication his card index, and other papers relating to the Tables. The many gentlemen who gave assistance in the revision of the Tables are also thanked for their help.

September 1921.   W. N. LING, *President, Scottish Mountaineering Club*

Cuillin Main Ridge, looking south from Bruach na Frithe.

INTRODUCTION

By SIR HUGH T. MUNRO, BART., F.R.G.S.

IN the Preface to the first number of the *S.M.C. Journal* it was correctly stated that there are more than three hundred mountains in Scotland whose height exceeds 3000 feet. The exact number cannot be determined, owing to the impossibility of deciding what should be considered distinct mountains. For instance, Braeriach and Cairn Toul are always counted as separate mountains, and so are the various peaks of the Cuillins, in Skye; and yet these are no more distinct than are Sròn an Isean or Stob Diamh from the two main peaks of Ben Cruachan, one and a half and two miles to the west. The names of these peaks, though, are not even given on the Ordnance sheet, but are generally included under the name Ben Cruachan.

In the following Tables, therefore, it has been thought best to include every " *top* " which attains an elevation of 3000 feet; while in the " separate mountain " column only such as may fairly be reckoned distinct mountains are numbered.

From the Tables it will be seen that whereas in the original Tables there were in all 538 tops of 3000 feet and upwards in height, of which 283 were considered distinct mountains, in the Revised Tables there are 543 and 276 respectively. The whole of these are situated in the Highlands, and all— with the exception of Ben More, in Mull, and the Cuillins and Blaven, in Skye—are on the mainland. The southernmost is Ben Lomond, in Stirling-shire; the northernmost is Ben Hope, in the north-west of Sutherlandshire; the easternmost is Mount Keen, above Loch Lee, between Forfarshire and Aberdeenshire; and the westernmost is Sgùrr na Banachdich, in the Cuillins, Skye; while on the mainland Ladhar Bheinn, in Knoidart, Inverness-shire, is the westernmost.

		1st Ed.	Revd.
In Stirlingshire	there is	1	1
,, Dunbartonshire	there are	3	3
,, Argyllshire (including one in Mull)	,,	56	57
,, Perthshire	,,	70	66
Between Argyll and Perthshire ..	,,	7	6
,, ,, ,, Inverness ..	,,	2	2
,, Perth and Inverness ..	,,	6	6
In Inverness (Mainland)	,,	147	143
,, ,, (Skye)	,,	15—162	21—164
Between Inverness and Ross-shire ..	,,	42	45
In Ross-shire	,,	95	95*
,, Sutherlandshire	,,	5	5
Between Aberdeen and Banffshire ..	,,	13	13
,, Inverness ,, ,, ..	,,	5	5
,, ,, ,, Aberdeen ..	,,	5	5
	Carry forward	472	473

* If Beinn Tarsuinn is included (pp. 36 and 52), 96.

			1st Ed.	Revd.
		Brought forward	472	473
· In Aberdeenshire	.. .. ..	there are	34	39
,, Banffshire ..	.. ..	,,	6	6
Between Aberdeen, Inverness and Perth		there is	1	1
,, ,, and Perth	..	there are	9	8
,, Perth and Forfarshire	..	there is	1	1
,, Aberdeen and Forfarshire ..		there are	7	7
In Forfarshire ..	.. .. ..	,,	8	8
			538	543

				1st Ed.	Revd.
From 3000 to 3049 inclusive	..	there are	92		71
,, 3050 ,, 3099	,,	..	,,	46—138	57—128*
,, 3100 ,, 3199	,,	..	,,	93	103
,, 3200 ,, 3299	,,	..	,,	99	88
,, 3300 ,, 3399	,,	..	,,	47	53
,, 3400 ,, 3499	,,	..	,,	43	48
,, 3500 ,, 3599	,,	..	,,	33	33
,, 3600 ,, 3699	,,	..	,,	37	38
,, 3700 ,, 3799	,,	..	,,	18	22
,, 3800 ,, 3899	,,	..	,,	12	12
,, 3900 ,, 3999	,,	..	,,	6	6
,, 4000 ,, 4406	,,	..	,,	12	12
				538	543

In the Tables the following natural grouping has been adopted, the revised numbers in each division being as under (old Nos. in parentheses):—

SECTION 1.—South of the Callander and Oban Railway .. (26) — 23

SECTION 2.—Enclosed by a line drawn by the railways from Killin Junction to Dunblane, Dunblane to Perth, and Perth to Ballinluig and Aberfeldy, and thence through Loch Tay to Killin Junction .. .. (3) 3

SECTION 3.—Enclosed by a line drawn from Tyndrum to Killin, thence to Ballinluig and Pitlochry, and by Lochs Tummel, Rannoch, and Laidon to Kingshouse, and back thence by road to Tyndrum .. .. (45) 44

SECTION 4.—Enclosed by a line drawn from Tyndrum to Kingshouse, down Glencoe, by Loch Linnhe to Oban, and back to Tyndrum .. .. (45) 46

SECTION 5.—Enclosed by a line drawn from Ballachulish up Glencoe to Kingshouse, and by Lochs Laidon, Rannoch, and Tummel to Pitlochry, thence up the Highland line to Newtonmore, and thence by Loch Laggan, Glen Spean, Glen Lochy, and Lower L. Eil to Ballachulish .. .. .. (74) 74

Carry forward .. 167 23

* With Beinn Tarsuinn, 57–129.

* With Beinn Tarsuinn, 29.　　† With Càrn a' Bhutha (pp. 40 and 53), 30.

0

EXPLANATION OF THE TABLES

COLUMN 1.—*Name.*—The Ordnance Survey spelling, even when obviously wrong, is always followed, as it is considered that the Tables to be of practical use must correspond with the standard maps. As is well known, the O.S. spelling is very incorrect, the same word being often spelt in different ways, even on the same sheet. The names, too, in the O.S. often differ from those locally used. Wherever a name is given on the O.S. map, however, it has been retained in the Tables.

In the Revised Tables, the highest point of the separate mountain is always put first, and its subsidiary peaks are grouped along with it; in a few cases, however, a neighbouring mountain might have equal claims to the top. Many names and spellings have been altered, but those of the original Tables are always indicated, either in italic, or, if lengthy, in a footnote, except where the identity of the name is not materially affected, as Mhòr for Mòr, Sgùrr for Sgòr, etc. The unsatisfactory nomenclature for nameless tops, " Top of Coire, etc.," has either been replaced by *N.*, *S.*, etc., *Top*, of its mountain, or by the Gaelic word " Stob " given in brackets thus, " [Stob] Coire, etc.," a more convenient form for actual use—though perhaps not quite a literal equivalent—until some definite nomenclature is adopted.

An * implies that the name is taken from the six-inch map, *but is not given on the one-inch* (7th *Series Edition*).

A † implies that the name is locally used, but is given neither on the six-inch nor one-inch maps. In all other cases the name is to be found on both the six- and one-inch maps. (See note on Cuillins, p. 42.)

A ‡ implies that a top did not appear in the original Tables.

COLUMN 2.—*Height.*—When not otherwise expressly stated, all the heights given are from the six-inch Ordnance Survey. Where only one height is given without qualification—as Ben Lomond, 3192—the six-inch and one-inch O.S. maps agree. When a height in smaller figures without parentheses precedes an exact height, the height is from the six-inch O.S., while the former is that given on the one-inch map, usually only a contour height—*e.g.* Aonach Meadhoin (3250) 3284—the true height as given on the six-inch map is 3284, while on the one-inch map there is only a 3250 contour. Where *only* a contour height is given—as Stùc Bheag (3250)—no figure is given on the six-inch map, and only a contour height on the one-inch. Heights altered in the Revised Tables can be found by reference to Table II.

" Ap." following after the height, signifies that it is only approximate, the authority in most cases being careful aneroid observations taken by Prof. Heddle, Mr Colin Phillip, Prof. Norman Collie, Mr Hinxman, or Sir Hugh

* With Beinn Tarsuinn and Càrn a' Bhutha, 545.

T. Munro. In the Revised Tables, these heights have not been altered unless (*a*) passed by Sir H. T. Munro; or (*b*) an O.S. height is now available; but some later measurements are given in the " Additional Notes".

COLUMN 3.—*County, etc.*—The county of Ross and Cromarty is given as " Ross." This column also shows the sheet-number of the 1-in. O.S. map containing the top.

COLUMNS 4 AND 5 respectively give the number in order of altitude of such hills as may fairly be considered separate mountains, and their distinct tops. [Since the Tables were first compiled in 1891, the former have been known among mountaineers as " Munros ".]

COLUMNS 6 AND 7—*Position.*—Positions of mountains are indicated by four figure map references as well as by bearings and distances from prominent points or places.

COLUMN 8.—*Best ascended from.*—When the nearest hotel lies at a considerable distance from the mountain, the name of a shooting-lodge or shepherd's cottage is given first; in such cases accommodation cannot be counted on. The names of two hotels are often given, that nearest the mountain being usually placed first. In the Revised Tables, additional starting points have often been added, as the advent of the motor has made many mountains much more accessible than formerly.

The distances and compass-bearings are only approximate, and the distances *are measured in a straight line on the map.* The compass-bearings *are those of the mountain from the hotel,* not those of the hotel from the mountain.

FOOTNOTES.—In the Revised Tables, some of the original notes have been deleted, being no longer required on account of additions to the Revised O.S. maps. Notes which did not appear in the original Tables, and which were not passed by Sir Hugh Munro, are given in brackets. Observations as regards height have been collated in the " Additional Notes " (p. 50).

The names corresponding to the initials used in the notes and " Additional Notes " are as follows:—

A.E.R., Rev. A. E. Robertson.
A.W.R., Mr A. W. Russell.
C.P., Mr Colin Phillip.
E.M.C., Dr Edred M. Corner.
F.S.G., Mr F. S. Goggs.
H.T.M., Sir H. T. Munro.
J.A.P., Mr J. A. Parker.
J.D., Mr J. Dow.
J.G.I., Mr J. Gall Inglis.
J.G.S., Mr J. G. Stott.
L.H., Mr L. Hinxman.
R.B., Mr Ronald Burn.
W.D., Mr W. Douglas.
J.R.C., Mr J. R. Corbett.
E.C.T., Mr E. C. Thomson.
R.G.I., Mr R. Gall Inglis.
J.N.C., Mr J. Norman Collie.

ABBREVIATIONS.—*B.*, Ben or Beinn; *bet.*, between; *C.*, Càrn; *Co.*, *Ch.*, Coire, Choire; *Cr.*, Creag; *Dist.*, district; *ft.*, feet; *fr.*, from; *in.*, inch; *m.*, mile; *yds.*, yards; *cont.*, contour; *Gl.*, glen; *hd.*, head; *Hot.*, Hotel; *I.*, Inn; *L.*, Loch; *Lo.*, Lodge; *M.*, Meall; *O.S.*, Ordnance Survey; *Sg.*, Sgùrr, Sgòr, etc.; *St.*, Stob; *S.M.C.*, Scottish Mountaineering Club.

In TABLE II. the " tops " are arranged and numbered in order of altitude, only those being numbered in the *first* column which may fairly be considered separate mountains.   Of these latter it will be seen that there are now only 276 as compared with 283 in the original Tables.*   Where heights are different in the original Tables, those of the latter are given in parentheses.   In the last column the number of the section is given, and with the help of this the reader will easily find the mountain in Table I.

Every endeavour has been made to secure accuracy and completeness.   It is inevitable that there should be some mistakes, but it is hoped they will not be found very numerous.   The decision as to what are to be considered distinct and separate mountains, and what may be counted as " tops", although arrived at after careful consideration, cannot be finally insisted on.

In the original compilation invaluable assistance was given by Mr Colin Phillip, whose extraordinary topographical knowledge of Scotland has probably never been equalled.

INDEX OF TOPS.—This includes all the names in both the original and Revised Tables, and also some conventional names used in tourist maps.

[NOTE ON CHANGES IN THE O.S. MAPS.—Since the publication of the original Tables in 1891, the six-inch O.S. map has been extensively revised, some counties being completely re-drawn in zinco-graphed quarter-sheets—which sometimes lack details shown in the older engraved sheets.   The one-inch map has been 4 times revised—the Original Series twice, with minor later additions.   The Third Revision, finished about 1926, was the ' Popular ' map.

In these revised maps, the heights of some tops have been increased, and those of others decreased, though in most cases only by trifling amounts, while some additional heights have been inserted, notably in Skye.

The mountain nomenclature has also been considerably modified.   Some entirely new names have been added, as well as a few of the " local names " of the original Tables; and in the one-inch maps many names and heights now appear that formerly were only given in the six-inch sheets. Many Tops have had their names entirely changed, and the spellings of others have been altered, sometimes to such an extent as to be hardly identifiable as the same name.

Changes made on the one-inch map in its First Revision (about 1895) have sometimes been again altered in the Second Revision (about 1905–1907).   Thus Meall Gruaidh of the original Survey maps is " Meall Graidhe " in the First Revision, and " Meall Greigh " in the Second Revision.   Another Revision of the six-inch map has been in progress for many years, but the mountain districts are said to have been hardly touched yet.

On the other hand, names altered in the First Revision are sometimes restored to the original form.   Thus Beinn Iutharn Mòr, Beinn Heasgarnich, and Ben Chonzie were altered to Ben Marn More, Beinn Theasgarnich, and Beinn a' Chonnaich, respectively, in the First Revision but appear in their original forms in the Second Revision.   (Third Revision, almost no change.)

The nomenclature of the six-inch Survey occasionally differs from that of the Second Revision one-inch maps: any important differences are indicated in the footnotes.   The Revised Tables follow throughout the six-inch map.—J.G.I.]

* If Beinn Tarsuinn is added, 277.

Speyside in winter.

TABLE I

The 3000-Feet Tops

(In the Revised Tables " [Stob] " represents " Top of ", " Top above ", etc., of the 1st edition.

NAME.	SECTION 1	HEIGHT.§	COUNTY. 1" O/S sht. No.		No. in order of Alt. Sep. Mt.	Top.	Map Ref.
Ben Lomond		3192	Stirling	53	178	322	37 03
Beinn Narnain		3036	Argyll	,,	256	490	27 06
Beinn Ime		3318	do.	,,	113	210	25 08
Ben Vane		3004	Dumbarton	,,	275	535	27 09
Beinn an Lochain	(2992)	3021 [1]	Argyll	,,	263	508	21 07
Ben Vorlich (South Top)		3092	Dumbarton	,,	220	420	29 12
do. (North Top)		3055	do.	,,	...	458	29 13
Beinn Buidhe		3106	Argyll	,,	211	398	20 18
Beinn a' Chleibh		3008	Arg., Perth	,,	272	527	25 25
Beinn Laoigh [2] (Ben Lui)		3708	do.	,,	25	48	26 26
Beinn Oss		3374	Perth ...	,,	99	183	28 25
Beinn Dubhchraig		3204	do. ...	,,	168	305	30 25
Beinn Chabhair		3053	do. ...	,,	242	461	36 18
An Caisteal		3265	do. ...	,,	142	256	37 19
Beinn a' Chroin (East Top)		3104	do. ...	,,	213	403	39 18
do. (West Top) ...	(3050)	3078	do. ...	,,	...	434	38 18
Beinn Tulaichean (*B. Tulachan*)		3099	do. ...	,,	216	416	41 19
Cruach Ardrain [14] (*Cr. Ardran*)		3428	do. ...	,,	83	158	40 21
Stob Garbh		3148	do. ...	,,	...	357	41 22
Ben More		3843	do. ...	,,	16	28	43 24
Am Binnein (Stobinian) ...	(3821)	3827	do. ...	,,	17	29	43 22
Stob Coire an Lochan [*Lochain, new* 1-in.]		3497	do. ...	,,	...	125	43 22
Meall na Dige		3140	do. ...	54	...	369	45 22

SECTION 2

NAME		HEIGHT	COUNTY		Mt.	Top.	Map Ref.
Ben Voirlich		3224	Perth ...	54	157	287	63 18
Stùc a' Chròin		3189	do. ...	,,	180	326	61 17
Ben Chonzie		3048	do. ...	48	247	474	77 30

SECTION 3

NAME		HEIGHT	COUNTY		Mt.	Top.	Map Ref.
Schichallion		3547	Perth ...	48	57	105	71 54
Càrn Mairg Range—							
Càrn Mairg		3419	do. ...	48	87	164	68 51
Meall Liath *	(3250)	3261	do. ...	,,	...	259	69 51
Meall a' Bhàrr [3]	(3250)	3315 ap.[3]	do. ...	,,	...	212	67 51
Creag Mhòr [4] (3100 *contour* ½" *O.S.*)		3200 ap.[4]	do. ...	,,	169	306	69 49
Meall Garbh do.	(3150)	3200 ap.[5]	do. ...	,,	171	308	64 51
Meall Luaidhe *	(3000)	3035 ap.[6]	do. ...	,,	...	492	65 51
An Sgòr *	(small 3000)	3002	do. ...	,,	...	541	64 51
Càrn Gorm [7]		3370	do. ...	,,	100	185	63 50
Ben Lawers Range—							
Ben Lawers		3984	do. ...	48	9	15	63 41
Creag an Fhithich * [8] ...	(3400)	3430	do. ...	,,	...	156	63 42
Meall Greigh (*Meall Gruaidh*) ...		3280	do. ...	,,	131	240	67 43
Meall Garbh		3661	do. ...	,,	33	59	64 43
An Stùc *	(3600)	3643	do. ...	,,	...	69	63 43
Beinn Ghlas	(3700)	3657 ap.[9]	do. ...	,,	37	63	62 40
Meall Corranaich	(3450)	3530 ap.[10]	do. ...	,,	61	112	61 41
Meall a' Choire Lèith		3033	do. ...	,,	260	495	61 43
Meall nan Tarmachan		3421	do. ...	,,	86	163	58 39
Meall Garbh *	(3250)	3369 ap.[11]	do. ...	,,	...	187	57 38
Beinn nan Eachan (West Top) ...	(3250)	3265 ap.[12]	do. ...	,,	...	255	56 38
do. (East Top)‡	(3000)	3110 ap.[6]	do. ...	,,	...	394	57 38
Meall Ghaordie		3407	do. ...	47	89	166	51 39
Stuchd an Lochain		3144	do. ...	,,	189	360	48 44
Sròn Chona Choirein * ...	(3000)	3031	do. ...	,,	...	496	48 44
Meall Buidhe (Garbh Mheall †) [13] ...		3054	do. ...	,,	241	460	49 49
do. (S.E. Top) ...	(3000)	3004	do. ...	,,	...	534	50 48

* *Named only on the 6-inch map.*   † *Local name, not given on either O.S. map.*
‡ *New top, not in the original Tables.*   § *The 1-in. height is given in parenthesis if different from 6-in*

[1] 150 yards N.E. of the 2995 point on the 1-in. map.   [2] The actual top is in Perthshire.   [3] [J. G. Inglis].   The name on the 1-in. map is ½m. S. of the top.   [4] Mr Colin Phillip.   On the 1-in. map the name is ½m. to E. of the top.   [The 3124 point on the 6-in. map is not the top, but almost certainly the col, J.G.I.].   [5] Mr Colin Phillip.   [The actual top is at the west end of the ridge; the point 3048 on the 1-in. map is only a point on the ridge, ½m. W. of the top, J.G.I.].   [6] [Mr J. G. Inglis].

TABLE I.
ARRANGED ACCORDING TO DISTRICTS.

Top. No.	Position.	Best Ascended From
	SECTION 1.	
322	2¾ m. N. by E. from Rowardennan ...	Rowardennan Inn, Loch Lomond, 2¾ m.;
490	2¼ m. N.W. of Arrochar	Arrochar, 2¼ m. [Aberfoyle, 9½ m.
210	3¾ m. N.W. from Arrochar	do. 3¾ m.
535	3¾ m. N.N.W. do.	do. 3¾ m.
508	Glencroe; 3 m. S.E. by E. from Cairndow	Cairndow, 3 m.; Arrochar, 5½ m.; St Cath-
420	2½ m. S.W. from Ardlui, Loch Lomond ...	Ardlui, 2½ m.; Arrochar, 5 m. [erines, 6 m.
458	2¼ m. do. do. ...	do. 2¼ m.
398	4 m. N. from head of Loch Fyne ...	Dalmally, 5¾ m.; Cairndow, 5 m.
527	1 m. S.W. by W. from Beinn Laoigh ...	Dalmally, 5 m.
48	6 m. E. from Dalmally	Tyndrum, 4¾ m.; Dalmally, 6 m.
183	1½ m. E.S.E. from Beinn Laoigh	Tyndrum, 4 m.
305	3¼ m. S.S.W. from Tyndrum	do. 3¼ m.
461	3½ m. E.N.E. from Ardlui, L. Lomond ...	Ardlui, 3¾ m.; Crianlarich, 4¾ m.
256	3¾ m. S. from Crianlarich	Crianlarich, 3¾ m.
403	4¼ m. S. by E. from Crianlarich	do. 4¼ m.
434	⅝ m. W. by S. of the East Top	do.
416	4 m. S.E. by S. from Crianlarich	do. 4 m.; Balquhidder, 7½ m.
158	3 m. S.E. by S. do.	do. 3 m.
357	2½ m. S.E. do.	do. 2½ m.
28	3 m. E. by S. do.	do. 3 m.; Balquhidder, 6¾ m.
29	1 m. S. from Ben More	do. 3½ m.; do. 6½ m.
125	½ m. S.E. by S. from Am Binnein ...	do. do.
369	1 m. E. from do. ...	do. 2 m.; do. 5½ m.
	SECTION 2.	
287	4 m. S.E. from Lochearnhead	Lochearnhead, 4 m.; Callander, 6¾ m.
326	1¼ m. S.W. from Ben Voirlich	do. 4¼ m.; do. 6 m.
474	Head of Glen Turret	Comrie, 5½ m.; Crieff, 8 m.
	SECTION 3.	
105	4 m. S.E. by E. from Kinloch Rannoch ...	K. Rannoch, 4 m.; Tummel Br., 4¼ m.; [Coshieville Inn, 5¼ m.
	Càrn Mairg Range—	
164	4 m. N.W. by W. from Fortingal ...	Fortingal, 4½ m.
259	½ m. E. by S. from Càrn Mairg ...	do. 4 m.
212	¾ m. W.N.W. from Càrn Mairg ...	do. 5¼ m.
306	3¼ m. W.N.W. from Fortingal	do. 3½ m.
308	2¼ m. W. from Càrn Mairg	do. 6½ m.; Kinloch Rannoch, 4½ m.
492	¾ m. S.E. by E. from Meall Garbh ...	do. do.
541	⅝ m. S.W. of Meall Garbh	do. 6¾ m.; do. 5 m.
185	4½ m. N.W. by W. of Invervar, Glen Lyon.	do. 7¼ m.; do. 5¾ m.
	Ben Lawers Range—	
15	Loch Tay, North Side	Killin, 6½m.; Lawers Inn, 3m.; Fortingal, 7½m.
156	½ m. N. from Ben Lawers	do. 7m.; do. 3¼m.; do. 7¼m.
240	2¾ m. N.E. by E. from Ben Lawers ...	do. 9m.; do. 2½m.; do. 4½m.
59	1½ m. N.N.E. from Ben Lawers ...	do. 8m.; do. 3½m.; do. 6¼m.
69	1 m. N. by E. do. ...	do. 7½m.; do. 3¼ m.; do. 6¾m.
63	⅞ m. S.W. do. ...	do. 5½ m.; do. 3¼m.
112	1¼ m. W. do. ...	do. 5½m.; do. 4m.
495	2 m. N.W. do. ...	do. 7¼m.; do. 5m.
163	3¾ m. N. by E. from Killin	do. 3¾ m.
187	½ m. S.W. from Meall nan Tarmachan ...	do. 3¼ m.
255	1 m. W.S.W. do. ...	do. 3¼ m.
394	¼ m. E. from Beinn nan Eachan, W. Top	do. 3¾ m.
166	Between Glen Lochay and Glen Lyon ...	Killin, 5½ m., N.W.
360	Between Glen Lyon and Loch Giorra ...	Fortingal 16½m; Br. of Orchy 12m; Tyndrum,
496	¾ m. E. by S. from Stuchd an Lochain ...	13m., both over the hills; Invermeran Lo., 5m.
460	Between Lochs Rannoch and Giorra ...	Bridge of Gaur, 4½ m.; Rannoch Station, 7m.
534	¾ m. S. by E. from Meall Buidhe ...	do. do.

7 [The 3000-ft. contour ¾m. to W.N.W. is only a shoulder, 3040 ft. approx., about 50 ft. above the col, J.G.I.]. 8 The summit is locally called Spicean nan Each. 9 Prof. Heddle. 10 Sir H. T. Munro. 11 Prof. Heddle. 12 Prof. Heddle. 13 ["Garbh Meall" on 1-in, map is ⅜m. to N.N.E. of the summit]. 14 [The "S.W. Top" of the 1st edition (3429 ft.). The "-77 point" (N.E. Top), conjectured to mean 3477 ft. is "3377" in the revised 6-in. map, and being evidently only a point on the rising ridge is now deleted].

NAME. SECT. 3—*Contd.*	HEIGHT. §	COUNTY. 1″ O/S sheet No.	Sep. Mt.	Top.	Map Ref.
Beinn Heasgarnich	3530	Perth ... 47	62	113	41 38
Stob an Fhir-Bhogha* ... ... (3300)	3381	do. ,,	...	178	41 37
Creag Mhòr	3387	do. ,,	94	175	39 36
Stob nan Clach* ... ... (3100)	3146	do. ,,	...	359	38 35
Beinn Chaluim (N. Top)	3354	do. ,,	104	195	38 32
do. (S. Top) ... ... (3250)	3236	do. ,,	...	280	38 31
Meall Glas[1]	3139	do. ,,	196	370	43 32
Beinn Cheathaich (*B. Dheiceach*)	3074	do. ,,	...	439	44 32
Sgiath Chùil ... ... (very small 3000)	3050 ap.[2]	do. ,, ,,	244	464	46 31
Meall a' Churain (*M. Chuirn*)	3007	do. ,, ,,	...	528	46 32
Beinn Dòrain (*B. Doireann*)	3524	Argyll ... ,,	63	115	32 37
Beinn an Dòthaidh ... ... (3267)	3283	do. ... ,,	129	237	32 40
Beinn Achaladair (N. Top) (*B. Achallader*) ...	3404[3]	Arg., Perth ,,	90	168	34 41
do. (S. Top)	3288	Arg., Perth ,,	...	233	34 42
Beinn a' Chreachain (*B. Creachan*) ...	3540	Perth ... ,,	60	109	37 44
Meall Buidhe ... ... (3150)	3193	Arg., Perth ,,	...	321	35 43
Beinn Mhanach (*Ben Vannoch*) ...	3125	Perth ... ,,	201	383	37 41
Beinn a' Chùirn	3020	Arg., Perth ,,	...	509	36 41

SECTION 4.

Cruachan Range—

NAME	HEIGHT. §	COUNTY. 1″ O/S sheet No.	Sep. Mt.	Top.	Map Ref.
Ben Cruachan (Main peak)	3689	Argyll ... 46	29	53	07 30
Stob Dearg†[4] (Taynuilt peak) ...	3611	do. ,,	...	82	06 30
Meall Cuanail	3004	do. 53	...	537	07 29
Drochaid Glas*	3312	do. 46	...	214	08 30
Stob Diamh†	3272	do. ,,	137	248	09 30
Stob Garbh†[5]	3215	do. ,,	...	297	09 30
Sròn an Isean†	3163	do. ,,	...	346	09 31
Beinn a' Chochuill	3215	do. ,,	163	298	11 32
Beinn Eunaich[6]	3242	do. 47	149	273	13 32
Beinn nan Aighean [*Aighenan, new* 1-in. *map.*]	3141	do. ,,	193	365	15 40
Ben Starav	3541	do. 46	59	108	12 42
Meall Cruidh* ... ... (3000)	3049	do. ,,	...	473	12 41
Stob Coire Dheirg* ... (3250)	3372	do. ,,	...	184	12 42
Glas Bheinn Mhòr	3258	do. 47	145	263	15 42
Stob Coir' an Albannaich ...	3425	do. ,,	84	159	16 44
Meall nan Eun	3039	do. ,,	254	487	19 44
Stob Ghabhar	3565	do. ,,	54	97	23 45
Stob a' Bhruaich Lèith ...	3083	do. ,,	...	429	20 46
Sròn a' Ghearrain ... (3200)	3240	do. ,,	...	277	22 45
Sròn nan Giubhas ... (3150)	3174	do. ,,	...	339	23 46
Aonach Eagach* ... (3250)	3272	do. ,,	...	249	23 45
Stob a' Choire Odhair	3058	do. ,,	240	456	25 46

Clach Leathad (Clachlet) Range—

NAME	HEIGHT. §	COUNTY. 1″ O/S sheet No.	Sep. Mt.	Top.	Map Ref.
Meall a' Bhùiridh	3636	do. ... 47	42	72	25 50
Clach Leathad (Clachlet) ...	3602	do. ,,	49	88	24 49
Mam Coire Easain* ...	3506	do. ,,	...	117	23 50
Crèise†[8] ... ... (3596)[7]	3600	do. ,,	...	90	24 50
Stob a' Ghlais Choire* ... (3150)	3207	do. ,,	...	304	24 51

Buachaille Etive Mòr—

NAME	HEIGHT. §	COUNTY. 1″ O/S sheet No.	Sep. Mt.	Top.	Map Ref.
Stob Dearg	3345	do. ... ,,	106	199	22 54
Stob na Doire* ... (3200)	3250 ap.[9]	do. ,,	...	269	20 53
Stob Coire Altruim† ...	3065	do. ,,	...	444	19 53
Stob na Bròige	3120	do. ,,	...	389	19 52

Buachaille Etive Bheag—

NAME	HEIGHT. §	COUNTY. 1″ O/S sheet No.	Sep. Mt.	Top.	Map Ref.
Stob Dubh[10] ... ... (3129)	3130[10]	do. ... ,,	199	377	18 53
Stob Coire Raineach* ...	3029	do. ,,	...	499	19 54
Bidean nam Bian	3766	do. ,,	23	38	14 54
Stob Coire nam Beith† ... (3600)	3621	do. ,,	...	80	14 54
Stob Coire nan Lochan (*St. Co. an Lochan*)	3657	do. ,,	...	65	14 54
Beinn Fhada: Stob Coire Sgreamhach†[11]	3497	do. ,,	...	124	15 53
do. (Centre Top)‡ ... (3000)	3120 ap.[12]	do. ,,	...	392	16 54
do. (N.E. Top)	3064	do. ,,	...	446	16 54
Sgòr na h-Ulaidh	3258	do. 46	144	262	11 51
Stob an Fhuarain*[13] ... (3000)	3160 ap.[13]	do. ,,	...	348	11 52
Beinn Fhionnlaidh	3139	do. ,,	197	371	10 49
Beinn Sgulaird	3059	do. ,,	239	454	05 46

* *Named only on the 6-inch map.*   † *Local name, not given on either O.S. map.*
‡ *New top, not in the original Tables.*   § *The 1-in. height is given in parenthesis if different from 6-in*

[1] Locally called Meall Glas *Mhòr.* [2] Prof. Heddle and Mr Colin Phillip. [3] 200 yards S.W. of the point 3399 on the 1-in. O.S. (old series). [4] Westernmost peak of Ben Cruachan. [5] About half way between Stob Diamh and "3091" on the 1-inch map. [6] The S. top of B. Eunaich, 3174 ft., is really only a shoulder. [7] 300 yards north of the 3600 contour. [8] Top between Mam Coire Easain and

Top. No.	POSITION. SECT. 3—*Contd.*	BEST ASCENDED FROM
113	1¾ m. S.E. from Loch Lyon	Invermeran Lo. (L. Lyon), 2¼ m.; Tyndrum *via*
178	½ m. S. from Beinn Heasgarnich ...	L. Lyon, 7¼ m.; Killin, *via* Glen Lochay, 10½m.
175	2¼ m. S.W. from Beinn Heasgarnich ...	Tyndrum, 5¼ m.; Br. of Orchy, 5½ m.; Crian-
359	⅔ m. S. by W. from Creag Mhòr ...	larich, 6½ m.; Kenknock (Gl. Lochay), 5 m.
195	3¾ m. E.N.E. from Tyndrum	Tyndrum, 3¾ m.; Crianlarich, 4¼ m.
280	½ m. S. of North Top	do. 3¾ m.; do. 4¾ m.
370	Between Glens Dochart and Lochay ...	Luib Sta. 3¾m.; Luib Hot, 4¾m.; Crianlarich 5¼m.
439	⅞ m. E.N.E. from Meall Glas	do. 3½m.; do. 4¼m.; do. 5¾m.
464	2½ m. N.N.W. from Luib Station ...	do. 2¼m.; or Hotel, 3¼m.; Crianlarich, 6½m.
528	½ m. N. of Sgiath Chùil	do. 3 m.; do. 3½ m.; do. 6½m.
115	Glen Orchy, 2 m. S.E. by E. of Br. of Orchy	Bridge of Orchy 2m.; Tyndrum, 4¾m.; Inveroran
237	do. 2¼ m. E.N.E. do.	do. 2¼m.; Inveroran, 3½m. [4m.
168	Head of Glen Lyon	do. 3¾ m.; do. 4½ m.
233	⅞ m. S.S.W. from the North Top ...	do. 3 m.; do. 4¼ m.
109	Head of Glen Lyon Hills	Inveroran, 6½ m.; Invermeran Lo., 2½ m.;
321	1 m. W.S.W. from Beinn a' Chreachain	Cashlie (Glen Lyon), 7½ m.
383	Head of Glen Lyon Hills	Inveroran, 6¼ m. across the hills; Tyndrum 7¼m.
509	¾ m. W. by S. from Beinn Mhanach ...	Invermeran Lo., 2¼m.; Cashlie (Gl. Lyon) 7¼m.
	SECTION 4.	
	Cruachan Range—	
53	Between Lochs Awe and Etive ...	Loch Awe Hotel, 4 m.; Taynuilt, 4¼ m.
82	½ m. W.N.W. of main peak	do. 4¼ m.; do. 3¾ m.
537	½ m. S. of do.	do. 3¾ m.; do. 4¼ m.
214	1 m. E. of do.	do. 3¼ m.; Taynuilt, 5 m.; Dalmally, 5¾m.
248	¾ m. E. by N. of Drochaid Glas ...	do. 2¾m.; do. 5¾ m.; do. 5m.
297	⅓ m. S. of Stob Diamh	do. 2½ m.; do. 5¾ m.; do. 5m.
346	N.E. spur of Cruachan	do. 2¾ m.; do. 6 m.; do. 5m.
298	3½ m. N. by W. from Loch Awe Hotel	do. 3½ m.; Dalmally, 5 m.
273	3½ m. N. by E. from do. ...	do. 3½ m.; do. 4 m.
365	2 m. S.E. from Ben Starav, Black Mt.	Doire nan Saor (Gl. Kinglas) 1¾m; Inveroran 8m.
108	East of Upper Loch Etive, do. ...	do. 3¾ m.; Kinlochetive, 1¾ m.; do. 9¼m.
473	⅜ m. S.S.E. of Ben Starav, do. ...	do. 3¼ m.; do. 2¼ m.; do. 9¼m.
184	⅓ m. E. do. do. ...	do. 3½ m.; do. 1¾ m.; do. 8¾m.
263	1¾ m. E. from Ben Starav, do. ...	Kinlochetive, 2¼ m.; Inveroran, 7¾ m.
159	3¼ m. E. by S. of Lochetivehead ...	Glenceitlin (Glen Etive), 2¾ m.; Inveroran, 6¾m.
487	5¾ m. W.N.W. from Inveroran	Inveroran, 5¾ m.
97	3¾ m. N.W. from Inveroran, Black Mt.	do. 3¾ m.; Kingshouse, 6 m.
429	1½ m. W. by N. from Stob Ghabhar ...	do. 5 m.; do. 6 m.
277	⅓ m. W. by N. do.	do. 4¼ m.; do. 6 m.
339	½ m. N.N.E. do.	do. 4 m.; do. 5¾ m.
249	⅓ m. E.S.E. do. (S.E. shoulder)	do. 3½ m.; do. 6 m.
456	1¾ m. E. by N. from Stob Ghabhar ...	do. 3 m. N.N.W.; Kingshouse, 5½ m.
	Clachlet Range—	
72	2¾ m. S. by W. from Kingshouse ...	Kingshouse (Black Mt.), 2¾ m.; Inveroran, 5¾m.
88	3½ m. S.S.W. do. ...	do. do. 3½ m. S.S.W.; do. 5½m.
117	½ m. N. from Clach Leathad ...	do. do. 3¼ m. S by W; do. 4¾m.
90	1 m. N. do. ...	do. do. 2¾ m. S by W; do. 6¼m.
304	¼ m. S. of Sròn na Crèise (2952, 1-in. OS)	do. do. 2¼ m. SW by S; do. 6¾m.
	Buachaille Etive Mòr—	
199	N.E. end of Buachaille Etive Mòr ...	do. do. 2¼ m. W by S; B. of Coe,[14] 8½m.
269	1¼ m. S.W. from Stob Dearg ...	do. do. 3 m. do. ; do. 7½m.
444	⅝ m. W.S.W. of Stob na Doire ...	do. do. 4¼ m. do. ; do. 7m.
389	S.W. end of Buachaille Etive Mòr ...	do. do. 4½ m. do. ; do. 7m.
	Buachaille Etive Bheag—	
377	Between Glencoe and Glen Etive ...	do. do. 5¼ m. do. ; do. 3¾m.
499	N.E. end of Buachaille Etive Bheag ...	do. do. 4¼ m. W. ; do. 4m.
38	Glencoe, 1½ m. S. of L. Achtriochtan ...	Br. of Coe,[14] 4 m.; Kingshouse, 7¼ m.
80	⅓ m. N.W. from Bidean nam Bian ...	do. 3¾ m.; do. 7½ m.
64	½ m. N.N.E. do. do. ...	do. 4 m.; do. 7¼ m.
124	¾ m. E.S.E. do. do. ...	do. 4¾ m.; do. 6½ m.
392	½ m. N.E. from Stob Coire Sgreamhach	do. 5 m.; do. 6 m.
446	¾ m. N.E. do. do. ...	do. 5 m.; do. 6¼ m.
262	Head of Glen Creran	do. 4½ m. S. by E.
348	½ m. N.E. from Sgòr na h-Ulaidh ...	do. 4½ m.
371	Head of Glen Creran	Glenceitlin (Glen Etive) 3½m.; B. of Coe,[14] 5½ m
454	2¾ m. E. from head of L. Creran ...	Creagan Inn, 5 m.; Appin Sta. and Hotel, 8 m.

Stob a' Ghlais Choire, 1st edn.: the point marked Sròn na Crèise on the 1-in, map (2952 ft.) is ¾m. farther N., and beyond Stob a Ghlais Choire. [9] Mr Colin Phillip. [10] [150 yards N.N.E. of the 3129 point on the 1-in. map]. [11] S.W. end of B. Fhada shoulder of Bidean; *Stob Coire Sgrenach*, 1st edn.]. [12] [Sir H. T. Munro]. [13] Prof. Heddle. Aonach Dubh a' Ghlinne (on both 1-in. and 6-in. maps) is the name of the ridge of which Stob an Fhuarain is the summit. [14] New Glencoe Hotel, at Carnoch.

NAME. SECT. 4—Contd.	HEIGHT. §	COUNTY.	1" O/S sheet No.	No. in order of Alt. Sep. Mt.	Top.	Map Ref.
Beinn a' Bheithir ...		Argyll ...	46	...	...	...
Sgòrr Dhearg ... 3362		do. ...	,,	103	191	05 56
Sgòrr Bhan† ...	3104	do. ...	,,	...	402	06 56
Sgòrr Dhonuill ...	3284	do. ...	,,	127	235	04 55
SECTION 5.						
Aonach Eagach (N. side of Glencoe)—						
Sgòr nam Fiannaidh ...	3168	Argyll ...	47	183	341	14 58
Stob Coire Lèith[1] ...	3080	do. ...	,,	...	432	15 58
Meall Dearg ...	3118	do. ...	,,	207	393	16 58
Am Bodach* ... (3000)	3085	do. ...	,,	...	426	17 58
Sgùrr Eilde Mòr (*Sgùrr na h-Eilde*) ...	3279	Inverness	,,	132	241	23 66
Binnein Mòr ...	3700	do. ...	,,	27	52	21 66
do. (S. Top) (*Top of Coire nan Laogh* (3450)	3475	do. ...	,,	...	133	21 65
Sgùrr Eilde Beag* (*Sg. na h-Eilde Beag*) (3150)	3140	do. ...	,,	...	368	21 65
Na Gruagaichean (*A' Gruagach*) ...	3442	do. ...	,,	77	148	20 65
do. (N.W. Top) ... (3400)	3404	do. ...	,,	...	169	20 65
Binnein Beag ...	3083	do. ...	,,	227	430	22 67
An Gearanach*[4] ... (3200)	3200 ap.[4]	do. ...	,,	172	310	18 66
An Garbhanach* ... (3150)	3200 ap.[4]	do. ...	,,	...	311	18 66
Stob Coire a' Chairn* ...	3219	do. ...	,,	159	293	18 66
Am Bodach (Mamore) ...	3382	do. ...	,,	96	177	17 65
Sgùrr a' Mhaim (*Sgòr*) ...	3601	do. ...	,,	50	89	16 66
Sgòr an Iubhair*[5]* ... (3250)	3300 ap.[5]	do. ...	,,	...	224	16 65
Stob Bàn (Mamore) ...	3274	do. ...	,,	135	245	14 65
Mullach nan Coirean (N.W. Top) ...	3077	do. ...	46	228	435	12 66
do. (S.E. Top) (*Top of Coire Dearg*) (3000)	3004	do. ...	47	...	536	13 65
Ben Nevis ...	4406	do. ...	,,	1	1	16 71
Càrn Dearg (S.W.) ...	3348	do. ...	,,	...	197	15 70
Càrn Dearg (N.W.) ...	3961	do. ...	,,	...	17	15 72
Carn Mòr Dearg ...	4012	do. ...	,,	7	12	17 72
Càrn Dearg Meadhonach ... (3850)	3873	do. ...	,,	...	22	17 73
Càrn Beag Dearg ... (3265)	3264	do. ...	,,	...	257	17 73
Aonach Mòr[6] ...	3999	do. ...	,,	8	13	19 73
[Stob] an Cul Choire* (*Top of ....*) (3500)	3580 ap.[7]	do. ...	,,	...	94	20 73
Stob Coire an Fhir Dhuibh* ...	3250 contour	do. ...	,,	...	272	20 73
Tom na Sròine *[9] ... (3000)	3015 ap.[8]	do. ...	,,	...	518	20 74
Aonach Beag ...	4060	do. ...	,,	6	10	19 71
[Stob] Coire Bhealaich * (*Top of ....*) (3600)	3644	do. ...	,,	...	68	20 70
Sgùrr a' Bhuic (*Sgòr ....*) ...	3165	do. ...	,,	...	344	20 70
Sgùrr Chòinnich Mòr (*Sgòr à ....*)	3603	do. ...	,,	48	87	22 71
Sgùrr Chòinnich Beag (do.) ...	3175 [10]	do. ...	,,	...	338	22 71
Stob Coire an Laoigh * ... (3560)	3659	do. ...	,,	34	60	24 72
Stob Coire an Easain ...	3545	do. ...	,,	...	107	23 72
Caisteal * [11] ... (3550)	3609	do. ...	,,	...	85	24 72
Stob Coire Cath na Sine*[12] (*... na Sgine*)(3500)	3529	do. ...	,,	...	114	24 72
Stob Choire Claurigh (S. Top) ...	3858	do. ...	,,	14	25	26 73
do. (N. Top)‡ ... (3500)	3719 ap.[13]	do. ...	,,	...	48	26 73
Stob a' Choire Lèith * ... (3500)	3627	do. ...	,,	...	77	25 73
Stob Coire Gaibhre * ... (3050)	3150 ap.[14]	do. ...	36	...	351	25 75
Stob Coire na Ceannain (*.... nan Ceann*)(3500)	3720 ap.[15]	do. ...	47	...	47	26 74
Stob Bàn (L. Treig District) ...	3217	do. ...	,,	162	295	26 72
Stob Coire Easain (*St. Ch. an Easain Mhoir*) ...	3658	do. ...	,,	35	61	30 73
Stob a' Choire Mheadhoin (*.... Mheadhonaiche*)	3610	do. ...	,,	47	84	30 73
Stob Coire Sgriodain (N. Top) ...	3211	do. ...	,,	165	301	35 74
do. (S. Top) (*Crags above Glac Bhan*) ...	3132	do. ...	,,	...	375	35 73
Chno Dearg ...	3433	do. ...	,,	80	153	37 74
Meall Garbh ... (3150)	3197	do. ...	,,	...	313	37 73
Beinn na Lap ...	3066	do. ...	,,	231	442	37 69
Càrn Dearg ... (3080)	3084	Inv., Perth	,,	225	427	41 66
Sgòr Gaibhre ... (3124)	3128	do. ...	,,	200	380	44 67
Sgòr Choinnich ...	3040	do. ...	,,	...	482	44 67
Beinn Eibhinn ...	3611	Inverness	,,	46	83	44 73
Mullach Coire nan Nead * ...	3025	do. ...	,,	...	505	43 73
Uinneag a' Ghlas-Choire * ... (3000)	3041	do. ...	,,	...	480	43 72

* *Named only on the 6-inch map.*   † *Local name, not given on either O.S. map.*
‡ *New top, not in the original Tables.*   § *The 1-in. height is given in parenthesis if different from 6-in.*

[1] Thus named, 6-in. map; on the 1-in., Meall Garbh.   [2] New " Glencoe Hotel." Carnoch.
[3] Tartan Hotel.   [4] [In the 1921 edition, An Garbhanach (at the S. end of the ridge) was made the top by a misunderstanding, but the actual summit is An Gearanach, fully ¼m. to the N., J.G.I.].   The *arete* between becomes extremely narrow [and precipitous]; both must be very near, if not over, 3250 ft., H.T.M.   [5] [Dr Corner.   The top is a small 3250 contour ¾m. S. of Sgurr a' Mhaim; highest figure on 6-in. map, 3066, ½m. farther S.].

Top No.	Position. SECT. 4—*Contd.*	Best Ascended From
	Beinn Bheithir—	
191	2¾ m. S. by E. of Ballachulish Hotel	Ballachulish Hotel, 2⅜ m.; Duror Inn, 4 m.
402	⅓ m. E.N.E. from Sgòrr Dhearg ...	do. 2⅜ m.; do. 4¼ m.
235	1 m. W. by S. do. ...	do. 2⅞ m.; do. 3 m.
	SECTION 5.	
	Aonach Eagach—	
341	West end of Aonach Eagach Ridge ...	B. of Coe,[2] 2½ m. to east; Kinlochleven,[3] 3½ m.
432	½ m. E. by N. of Sgòr nam Fiannaidh	do. 3 m. do. 3 m.
393	1⅜ m. E. of do.	do. 4 m. do. 2¾ m.
426	½ m. E.S.E. from Meall Dearg ...	do. 4¼ m. do. 2½ m.
241	Above L. Eilde Mòr, Mamore Forest	Kinlochleven,[3] 3¾ m.; Fort William, 9½ m.
51	Between Glen Nevis and L. Eilde Mòr	do. 3¼ m. N.E. by N.; Fort W., 9½ m.
133	½ m. S. from Binnein Mòr	do. 3 m.; do. 8½ m.
368	Top of ridge ⅞m. S.E. by S. fr. Binnein Mòr	do. 3 m.; do. 9 m.
148	1 m. S.W. from Binnein Mòr	do. 2½ m.; do. 8¼ m.
169	¼ m. N.W. from Na Gruagaichean ...	do. 2½ m.; do. 8 m.
430	Head of Glen Nevis, Mamore Forest ...	do. 4¼ m.; do. 8½ m.
310	1½ m. S. from Steall, Glen Nevis ...	do. 3 m.; do. 7 m.
311	⅓ m. S. from An Gearanach	do. 3¼ m.; do. 6¾ m.
292	⅞ m. N.E. fr. Am Bodach, Mamore Forest	do. 2¾ m.; do. 7 m.
177	Bet. Glen Nevis and head of L. Leven	Kin'leven, 2 m.; Ft. W., 7¼ m.; Polldubh, 3¼m.
89	Glen Nevis, Mamore Forest	do. 3¼ m.; do. 6 m.; do. 2¾ m.
224	¾ m. S. from Sgùrr a' Mhaim	do. 2½ m.; do. 6½ m.; do. 3 m.
245	Glen Nevis, Mamore Forest	do. 3¼ m.; do. 6 m.; do. 2 m.
435	do. do.	do. 4¾ m.; do. 5 m.; do. 2 m.
536	¾ m. S.E. from N.W. Top	do. 4 m.; do. 5½ m.; do. 2 m.
1	Lochaber	Fort W., 4½ m.; End Gl. Nevis Road, 1¼ m.
197	S.W. Spur of Ben Nevis, 1 m. S.W. ...	do. 3¾ m.; do. do. 1 m.
17	N.W. do. ¾ m. N.W. ...	do. 4 m.; do. do. 2 m.
12	Between Ben Nevis and the two Aonachs	do. 5 m.; do. do. 2 m.
22	½ m. N.N.W. from Càrn Mòr Dearg ...	do. 4¾ m.; do. do. 2½ m.
257	1 m. do. do.	do. 4½ m.; do. do. 2¾ m.
13	2 m. N.E. by E. from Ben Nevis ...	Spean Br., 5¾ m.; Ft. W., 5¾ m.; do. 3 m.
94	⅜ m. E. by N. from Aonach Mòr ...	do. 5½ m.; do. 6¼ m.; do. 3¼ m.
271	1 m. E.N.E. do. ...	do. 5¼ m.; do. 6½ m.; do. 3¾ m.
518	1½ m. N.E. do. ...	do. 4½ m.; do. 6½ m.; do. 4¼ m.
10	2 m. E. from Ben Nevis	do. 6½ m.; do. 6¼ m.; do. 2½ m.
68	½ m. S.E. from Aonach Beag, Lochaber	do. 6¾ m.; do. 6½ m.; do. 2½ m.
344	1 m. S.E. by S. do. , above Gl. Nevis	Fort W. *via* Glen Nevis, 6¾ m.; do. 2½ m.
87	3¾ m. E. fr. B. Nevis, North side of do.	Spean Br., 5½ m.; Roy Br., 5¾ m.; Ft. W., 8 m.
338	⅝ in. W.S.W. from Sgùrr Chòinnich Mòr	do. 6¾ m.; do. 7¼ m.; do. 7¾ m.
60	⅓ m. E. by S. from Stob Coire an Easain	do. 5¾ m.; do. 5¾ m.; do. 8¾ m.
107	4¼m. E. by N. of B. Nevis, N. side Gl. Nevis	do. 5½ m.; do. 5¾ m.; do. 8 m.
85	¾ m. E.N.E. from Stob Coire an Easain	Roy Bridge, 5½ m.; Spean Bridge, 5¾ m.
114	⅓ m. E. by N. from Caisteal	do. 5¼ m.; do. 5½ m.
25	4½ m. S. from Roy Bridge	do. 4½ m.; do. 5½ m.
47	⅓ m. N. from Stob Choire Claurigh ...	do. 4¼ m.; do. 5¼ m.
77	⅓ m. W. by S. do. ...	do. 4¾ m.; do. 5½ m.
351	1¼ m. N. do. ...	do. 3½ m.; do. 4½ m.
46	⅓ m. N.N.E. do. ...	do. 4¼ m.; do. 5¼ m.
295	4 m. N.W. by N. from head of L. Treig	Roy B. 5½m.; Tulloch St. 7¼m.; Corrour[17] 6¾m.
61	1½ m. W. from Loch Treig	do. 5½m.; do. 5½m.; do. 5m.
84	⅜ m. N.E. from Stob Coire Easain ...	do. 5½m.; do. 4¾m.; do. 5¼m.
301	¾ m. E. from Loch Treig	Tulloch St., 3¾ m.; Roy Bridge, 6¾ m.
375	⅓ m. S.S.E. of Stob Coire Sgriodain ...	do. 4 m.; do. 7¼ m.
153	2 m. E. from Loch Treig	do. 4¼ m.; Moy[16] 6 m.; Roy Br. 8 m.
313	Shoulder ¾ m. S.W. by W. of Chno Dearg	do. 5 m.; do. 6¾ m.; do. 8 m.
442	1 m. N.W. from Loch Ossian	Corrour Siding, 2¼ m. N.N.E.
427	1½ m. S.E. do.	do. 3¾ m.; Rannoch Sta., 5¼ m.
380	Between Lochs Ossian and Ericht ...	do. 5½ m.; do. 6 m.
482	⅝ m. N. from Sgòr Gaibhre	do. 5½ m.; do. 6¾ m.
83	3 m. W. by N. from Ben Alder	Moy[16] 6m. S.S.E.; Dalw. 13m.; Corrour[17] 7¼m.
505	1m. W. from Beinn Eibhinn	do. 5¾m. S.S.E.; do. 14½m.; do. 6¼m.
480	¾ m. W.S.W. do.	do. 6¼m.; do. 14¼m.; do. 6½m.

Aonach an Nid, 1m. N. of Aonach Mòr (3374 ft. 6-in. map), is really on a shoulder, and not to be considered a top, H.T.M. [7] [Prof. Heddle; name of burn on 1-in. map, Allt a' Chùl Choire]. [8] [Dr Corner]. [9] The 3000-ft. contour (1-in. map) is about ¾m. S. of *name* Tom na Sròine on the 6-in. map. [10] [200 yds. N.E. of the 3108 point on the 1-in. map] (old series). [11] W. end of the 3500 contour. [12] E. end of the 3500 contour. [13] [Dr Corner]. [14] Mr Colin Phillip. [15] Prof. Heddle. [16] Moy (Kingshouse), 1½m. from foot of L. Laggan, has no inn. [17] Corrour Siding W. Highland Railway.

NAME. SECT. 5—*Contd.*	HEIGHT. §	COUNTY. 1″ O/S sheet No.	No. in order of Alt. Sep. Mt.	Top.	Map Ref.
Aonach Beag (Alder District) ... ... (3647)	3646	Inverness	47	39	66	45 74
Geal-Chàrn * 2 (N.W. of B. Alder) ... (3650)	3688	do.	,,	30	54	47 74
Sgòr Iutharn 3 * (*Sgòr Iutharna*) ... (3250)	3300 ap.3	do.	,,	...	222	49 74
Càrn Dearg (Alder District)	3391	do.	36	93	173	50 76
Diollaid a' Chàirn ... ... (3000)	3029	do.	,,	...	500	48 75
Beinn a' Chlachair (*B. a' Clachair*)	3569	do.	,,	53	96	47 78
Creag Pitridh (*Creag Peathraich*)	3031	do.	,,	261	497	48 81
Mullach Coire an Iubhair4* (Geal Càrn, *new* 1-in. *map*	3443	do.	,,	76	147	50 81
Sròn Garbh ... ... (3350)	3320 ap.5	do.	,,	...	209	51 81
Ben Alder	3757	do.	47	24	39	49 71
Beinn Bheòil	3333	do.	,,	111	204	51 71
Sròn Coire na h-Iolaire	3128	do.	,,	...	382	51 70
Sgairneach Mhòr (*Mòr*) ... (3160)	3210 ap.6	Perth	48	166	302	59 72
Beinn Udlamain (*B. Udlaman*)	3306	Inv., Perth	,,	118	217	58 74
A' Mharconaich7 (*Marcaonach*) ... (3174)	3185	Inverness	37	181	330	60 76
Geal Chàrn (L. Ericht)	3005	do.	,,	274	533	59 78
SECTION 6.					
Beinn a' Chaoruinn, (S. Top)	3437	Inverness	36	79	151	38 84
do. (N. Top)	3422	do.	,,	...	162	38 85
Creag Meaghaidh Range—					
Creag Meaghaidh	3700	do.	,,	26	50	41 87
An Cearcallach	3250	do.	,,	...	268	42 85
Meall Coire Choille-rais (*Coille na Froise*)(3250)	3299	do.	,,	...	225	43 86
Creag Mhòr 8 ... ... (3450)8	3496	do.	,,	...	126	44 87
Puist Coire Ardair*9(*Crags above Coire Ard Dhoire*)	3591	do.	,,	...	91	43 87
[Stob] Poite Co. Ardair* (W. Top10) (*Creag an Lochain*) (3250)	3460	do.	,,	70	137	43 89
do. E. Top10 (*Crom Leathad*) (3400)	3441	do.	,,	...	149	43 89
Sròn Garbh Choire 11	3250 contour11	do.	,,	...	272	44 90
Càrn Liath	3298	do.	,,	122	226	47 90
Meall an-t-Snaim 12 *	3180	do.	,,	...	334	46 90
A' Bhuidheanach (*Buidh' Aonach*) centre top	3177	do.	,,	...	336	48 90
[Stob] Choire Dhuibh (*Top Co. Dubh*) (small 3000)	3002	do.	,,	...	540	49 91
Monadh Liadh Mountains—					
Càrn Dearg, (N.W. Top)	3093	do.	37	219	419	63 02
do. (S.E. Top) ... ... (3000)	3025	do.	,,	...	504	63 01
Càrn Bàn (*Càrn Mairg*)	3087	do.	,,	224	425	63 03
Snechdach Slinnean * ... ... (3000)	3011	do.	,,	...	524	62 02
Càrn Ballach (N.E. Top)13 ... (3000)	3020 ap.13	do.	,,	264	510	62 02
Càrn Sgùlain	3015	do.	,,	268	516	68 05
A' Chailleach	3045	do.	,,	248	476	68 04
Geal Chàrn	3036	do.	,,	257	491	56 98
SECTION 7.					
Sròn a' Choire Ghairbh	3066	Inverness	36	232	443	22 94
Meall na Teanga (*M. an Teanga*) ... (2950)	3050 ap.14	do.	,,	245	467	22 92
Gaor Bheinn or Gulvain, (N. Top) 15	3224	Arg., Inv.	35	156	286	00 87
do. (S. Top) 15	3148	do.	,,	...	356	99 86
Sgùrr Thuilm (*Sgòr Choileam*)	3164	Inverness	,,	186	345	94 88
Sgùrr nan Coireachan (Glenfinnan) ... (3136)	3133	do.	,,	198	374	90 88
Sgùrr na Ciche (*Sgòr ....*)	3410	do.	,,	88	165	90 96
Garbh Chiòch Mhòr ... ... (3350)	3365 ap.17	do.	,,	...	190	90 96
do. Bheag * ... ... (3100)	3100 ap.17	do.	,,	...	410	91 96
Sgùrr nan Coireachan (Glen Dessary) ...	3125	do.	,,	202	384	93 95
Sgùrr Mòr	3290	do.	,,	125	232	96 98
Gairich (*Scour Gairoch*)	3015	do.	,,	267	515	02 99
Meall Buidhe	3107	do.	,,	209	396	85 99
Luinne Bheinn	3083	do.	,,	226	428	87 00

* *Named only on the 6-inch map.*   † *Local name not given on either O.S. map.*
‡ *New top, not in the original Tables.*   § *The 1-in. height is given in parenthesis if different from 6-in.*

1 Moy (Kingshouse), 1½m. from foot of L. Laggan, has no inn.   2 Although unnamed and only a 3650 contour on 1-in. map, Geal Chàrn is culminating point of the large range immediately to the N. of B. Alder.   3 [Estimate from hill-shaded 1-in. map. Seen end on, Sgòr Iutharn is a "lancet edge." Having stood on the top of it, and of every top in the district, I fancy it must be fully 3400 feet, and standing well out is almost worthy to be considered a separate mountain, H.T.M.].   4 This name appears only on the 6-in. map; on revised 1-in. map name is Geal Chàrn.   5 [Estimate from hill-shaded 1-in. map; new 3350 contour confirms. On the 6-in. map ' 3206 ' is merely a point on a long ridge, the actual top of which is about ¼m. further S.W.].   6 [Estimate from hill-shaded 1-in. map; the actual top is at the edge of the cliffs, ¼m. N.E. of 3160 point.].   7 Bruach nan Iomairean (3175),

Top No.	Position.	Best Ascended From
	SECT. 5—*Contd.*	
66	2¾ m. W.N.W. from Ben Alder ...	Moy,[1] 5¾ m. S.S.E.; Dalwhinnie, 12 m.
54	1 m. E.N.E. of Aonach Beag, B. Alder For.	do. 5¾ m. S.E. by S.; do. 12 m.
222	2 m. E. from do. do.	do. 6¾ m.; do. 11¼ m.
173	3 m. N. from Ben Alder	do. 6½ m.; do. 9¾ m.
500	1¼ m. W.S.W. from Càrn Dearg ...	do. 6 m.; do. 11 m.
96	4¼ m. N.N.W. from Ben Alder	do. 4¼ m.; L. Laggan Inn, 8 m.; Dalw. 11m.
497	6 m. N. from do.	do. 4¼ m.; do. 5¾ m.; do. 9¾m.
147	1 m. E. from Creag Pitridh [Iubhair }	do. 5 m.; do. 5½ m.; do. 8¾m.
209	Shoulder ½m. E. by S. fr. Mul. Co. an }	
39	W. side of Loch Ericht	do. 8¼ m.; Dalwhinnie Hotel, 11¾ m.
204	1¼ m. E. from Ben Alder	Dalwhinnie Hotel, 11 m.
382	¾ m. S.S.W. from Beinn Bheòil ...	do. 11½ m.
302	3 m. W. from Dalnaspidal Station ...	Dalnaspidal St., 3 m.; Dalwhinnie Hot., 7¼ m.
217	4 m. W. do. ...	do. 4 m.; do. 7¼ m.
330	3 m. N.W. by W. do. ...	do. 3 m.; do. 5½ m.
533	4½ m. S.W. by S. from Dalwhinnie ...	Dalwhinnie Hotel, 4½ m.
	SECTION 6.	
151	North side of Glen Spean	Moy [1] (L. Laggan), 2½ m.; Roy Bridge, 7½ m.
162	¾ m. N. by W. from S. top	do. 3 m.; do. 7½ m.
	Creag Meaghaidh Range—	
50	3 m. N.N.W. from foot of Loch Laggan	Moy[1] (L. Laggan), 3 m. N.; L. Laggan I., 7 m.
268	1⅓ m. S. by E. from Creag Meaghaidh	do. 1¾ m.; do. 7¼ m.
225	1 m. S.E. do. ...	do. 2½ m.; do. 6 m.
126	1½ m. due E. do. ...	do. 3¼ m.; do. 5¾ m.
91	1 m. do. do. ...	do. 3¼ m.; do. 6 m.
137	1 m. N.E. do. ...	do. 3¾ m.; do. 6½ m.
149	⅝ m. E.N.E. from [Stob] Poite Coire Ar.	do. 4¼ m.; do. 5¾ m.
272	1⅜ m. E.N.E. do. ...	do. 4¾ m.; do. 5¼ m.
226	3½ m. W. from Loch Laggan Inn ...	L. Laggan Inn, 3½ m.; Moy, 5¾ m.
334	⅞ m. W. by N. from Càrn Liath ...	do. 4½ m.; do. 5¼ m.
336	⅓ m. E.N.E. do. ...	do. 3¼ m.; do. 6 m.
540	1¾ m. N.E. by N. do. ...	do. 2½ m. W.N.W.
	Monadh Liadth Mountains—	
419	5½ m. W.N.W. from Newtonmore ...	Newtonmore, 5½ m.
504	½ m. S.E. from N.W. Top	do. 5¼ m.
425	5¾ m. W.N.W. from Newtonmore ...	do. 5¾ m.
524	⅔ m. W.S.W. from Càrn Bàn	do. 6¼ m.
510	1½ m. N.E. do.	do. 5½ m.
516	4½ m. N.N.W. from Newtonmore ...	do. 4½ m.
476	3¾ m. N.W. do. ...	do. 3¾ m.
491	9¾ m. W. do. ...	L. Laggan Inn, 6 m.; Newtonmore, 9¾ m.
	SECTION 7.	
443	2 m. W. of L. Lochy, Caledonian Canal	Tomdoun (5¾ m.); Inverg. (7 m.), or Gairlochy.
467	1¾ m. S. by W. of Sròn a' Choire Ghairbh	do. (6¾ m.), do. (7¾ m.), do. (6 m.)
286	Between the heads of L. Eil and L. Arkaig	Glenfinnan,[16] 7½ m.; Corpach, 8¾ m.
356	¾ m. S.S.W. from N. Top	do. 7¼ m.; do. 8½ m.
345	Head of Glenfinnan	Glenfinnan,[16] 5 m. N.N.E.
374	do. 2¼ m. W. of Sgùrr Thuilm	do. 4¼ m.
165	2½ m. N.E. by N. from head of L. Nevis }	Kinlochquoich, 4½ m.; Glendessary (1½m. NNW of head of L. Arkaig), 4¾ m.; Tarbet (Loch Nevis), 7¼ m. (no inn); Kinlochhourn, 7 m.
190	½ m. S.E. from Sgùrr na Ciche ... }	
410	1 m. E.S.E. do. ... }	
384	N. of Glen Dessary, head of Loch Arkaig	Glendes'y, 3m.; Tarbet (L. Nev.), 9m.; do. 6¾m.
232	1½ m. S. from head of Loch Quoich ...	Kinlochquoich, 1½ m.; Tomdoun Inn, 12 m.
515	1½ m. S. from middle of do. ...	Tomdoun Inn, 8 m.; Kinlochquoich, 4 m.
396	2 m. N.N.W. from head of L. Nevis ...	Inverie, 5 m. E.
428	3½ m. N. do. do. ...	do. 6¼ m.; Kinlochhourn, 6¼ m.

a short ½m. S. by W., is merely a shoulder of A'Mharconaich. [8] The summit named Creag Mhòr (3496 ft.) on the 6-in. map is about ⅓m. N. of the *name* Creag Mhòr on the 1-in. map; [the very small 3500 contour appears on the Revised 1-in. " Outline " map, but is omitted in the later red-contour issue (also in new 1-in. map). [9] Mrs Grant, in *Letters from the Mountains*, 1806, speaks of the whole range as the " lofty Corryarder." [10] [The E. Top] is the point marked 3441 at N.E. end, and [the W. Top] is S.W. end of large 3250 contour on 1-in. map (Old Series), commencing ¾m. N.E. of Creag Meaghaidh: [the names Crom Leathad and Creag an Lochain on the O.S. maps are both ⅜m. away from these tops, and apparently refer to quite different features]. [11] The small 3250 contour is ½m. E. of the *name* Sròn Garbh Choire on 1-in. and 6-in. maps. [12] Top of Coire a' Chaoruinn, 1st edn. [13] [Mr J. G. Inglis]. [14] Prof. Heddle, with careful aneroid measurements, and levels from other hills. [15] N. top locally called Gulvain Mòr, the S. top Gulvain Beag. [16] Stagehouse Hotel. [17] Prof. Heddle.

NAME — SECT. 7—Contd.	HEIGHT. §	COUNTY 1" O/S sheet No.		Sep. Mt.	Top.	Map Ref.
Ladhar Bheinn	3343	Inverness	35	107	200	82 04
Stob a' Choire Odhair (3000)	3138 [1]	do.	,,	...	372	83 04
Ben Sgritheall (Sgriol)	3196	do.	,,	174	315	83 12
do. (N.W. Top) (3000)	3039	do.	,,	...	485	83 13
The Saddle (3314)	3317	Inv., Ross	,,	114	211	93 13
do. (W. Top) (3150)	3196	do.	,,	...	316	92 12
Sgùrr Leac nan Each	3013	do.	,,	...	522	91 13
Spidean Dhomhnuill Bhric (*Sg. na Creige*)	3082	do.	,,	...	431	92 12
Sgùrr na Forcan † (3050)	3100 ap.[3]	Ross	,,	...	409	94 13
Sgùrr na Creige[4] (*Top ½m. N. of The Saddle*) (3100)	3100 ap.[4]	do.	,,	...	413	93 13
Sgùrr na Sgine	3098	Inv., Ross	,,	218	418	94 11
Faochag (*Fraochag*) (3000)	3010 ap.[5]	Ross	,,	...	525	95 12
Sgùrr a' Mhaoraich (*Sg. a' Mhoraire*)	3365	Inverness	,,	102	189	98 06
Am Bàthaich (3000)	3055 ap.[5]	do.	,,	...	459	99 07
Sgùrr a' Mhaoraich Beag * (3100)	3101	do.	,,	...	408	97 06
Gleouraich (*Gleourach*)	3395	do.	,,	92	172	04 05
do. (E. Top) (3250)	3291	do.	,,	...	231	04 04
Spidean Mialach	3268	do.	,,	139	252	06 04
Creag a' Mhàim	3102	Ross	,,	21'5	407	08 07
Druim Shionnach (*Drum Sionnach*) (3200)	3222	do.	,,	158	289	07 07
Maol Chinn-dearg—						
Aonach air Chrith	3342	Inv., Ross	,,	108	201	05 08
Maol Chinn-dearg[6] (*Maol Cheann-dearg*) W. top	3214	do.	,,	164	299	03 08
Sgùrr an Doire Leathain (3250)	3272	do.	,,	138	250	01 09
Sgùrr an Lochain	3282	do.	,,	130	239	00 10
Creag nan Damh	3012	do.	,,	271	523	98 11

SECTION 8.

NAME	HEIGHT. §	COUNTY 1" O/S sheet No.		Sep. Mt.	Top.	Map Ref.
Five Sisters, or *Beinn Mhòr*[7] *Range—*						
Sgùrr Fhuaran[8] (Scour Ouran)	3505	Ross	35	65	119	97 16
Sgùrr na Càrnach[8] (3250)	3270	do.	,,	...	251	97 15
Sgùrr na Ciste Duibhe[8]	3370	do.	,,	101	186	98 14
Sgùrr nan Spainteach † (3100)	3129	do.	,,	...	379	99 14
Sàileag (3100)	3124	do.	,,	203	386	01 14
Sgùrr a' Bhealaich Dheirg	3378	Inv., Ross	,,	97	180	03 14
Aonach Meadhoin † (3250)	3284	do.	,,	128	236	04 13
Sgùrr an Fhuarail (*Càrn Fuaralach*)	3241	do.	,,	...	276	05 13
Ciste Dhubh	3218	do.	,,	160	293	06 16
Mullach Fraoch-choire[9] (Centre Top)	3614	Inverness	,,	45	81	09 17
do. (N.E. Top) (3400)	3435	do.	,,	...	152	10 17
do. (S. Top) (*Coire Odhar*)	3295	Inv., Ross	,,	...	227	09 16
A' Chràlaig (*Garbh-leac*) (*Cralic*)	3673	do.	,,	31	55	09 14
A' Chìoch (3100)	3050 ap.[5]	Inverness	,,	...	468	10 15
Tigh Mòr na Seilge (S.S.W. Top) (*Tigh Mòr*)	3285	do.	,,	126	234	13 15
do. (Centre Top)	3276	do.	,,	...	242	13 15
do. (N.N.E. Top)	3045	do.	,,	...	475	14 16
Sàil Chaoruinn (3000)	3025 ap.[5]	do.	,,	...	506	14 15
Sgùrr nan Conbhairean (3634)	3635	Inv., Ross	,,	43	73	13 14
Drochaid an Tuill Easaich * (3250)	3300 ap.[5]	do.	,,	...	223	12 13
Creag a' Chaoruinn †	3260[10]	do.	,,	...	261	13 13
Càrn Ghluasaid	3140	do.	,,	194	366	14 12
A' Ghlas-bheinn	3006	Ross	26	273	531	00 23
Beinn Fhada (Ben Attow)—						
Beinn Fhada (3385)	3383	Inv., Ross	35	95	176	01 19
Ceum na h'-Aon Choise * (3050)	3150 ap.[11]	Ross	,,	...	354	00 19
Sgùrr a' Dubh Doire † (*Sgòr ....*) (3050)	3100 ap.[12]	Inv., Ross	,,	...	411	03 18
Sgùrr nan Ceathreamhnan (Centre Top[17])	3771	do.	26	22	36	05 22
do. (W. Top) (3700)	3736	do.	,,	...	43	05 22
do. (E. Top ‡) (3150)	3150 ap.[13]	do.	,,	...	353	05 22
[Stob] Coire nan Dearcag (*Top of ....*) (3050)	3089	do.	,,	...	421	07 22
Stùc Mòr † (3250)	3496 ap.[14]	Ross	,,	...	127	05 23
Stùc Bheag † (3250)	contour [15]	do.	,,	...	270	05 23
Creag nan Clachan Geala * (3250)	3282	do.	,,	...	238	04 23

* *Named only on the 6-inch map.*　　† *Local name, not given on either O.S. map.*
‡ *New top, not in the original Tables.*　　§ *The 1-in. height is given in parenthesis if different from 6-in.*

[1] Admiralty chart; no height on O.S. maps.　　[2] [Shiel Inn now closed (1949)].　　[3] Mr Colin Phillip, levels from The Saddle.　　[4] [Estimate from hill-shaded 1-in. map; name is ½m. N. of the top, 1-in. map: local name, Sgùrr Nid na h-Iolaire, A.E.R. In 1st edn., " Sg. na Creige " was Top No. 431].　　[5] [Dr Corner].　　[6] " Maol Chinn-dearg " is applied to the whole ridge—both to this top and Aonach air Chrith.　　[7] [This name, which formerly appeared on the 1-in. map, was deleted in the 1906 Revision;

Top No.	POSITION. **SECT. 7.**—*Contd.*	BEST ASCENDED FROM
200	Between Lochs Nevis and Hourn, Knoydart	Inverie, 4¼m; or Arnisdale, Loch Hourn, by ferry
372	⅓ m. E.N.E. from Ladhar Bheinn ...	do. 4½ m.; do. do. [4¼ m.
315	N. side of Loch Hourn	Arnisdale, 1½ m.; Glenelg, 4½ m.
485	¼ m. N.N.W. from Main Top	do. 1¾ m.; do. 4¼ m.
211	Between h'ds of Lochs Duich and Hourn }	Shiel Br.[2] 3¾m.; Kin'hourn 4¼m.; Glenelg 8¾m.;
316	½ m. W.S.W. of The Saddle ... }	Cluanie[18], 8¾m.
522	1¼ m. W. do.	Shiel Br. 3¾m.; Kin'hourn 4¾m.; Glenelg, 8m.
431	¾ m. W. by S. do.	do. 3¾m.; do. 4¼m.; do. 8m.
409	⅓ m. E. do.	do. 3¾m.; do. 4m.; do. 9½m.
413	½ m. N. do.	do. 3m.; do. 4¾m.; do. 8¾m.
418	1¼ m. S.E. by S. from The Saddle ...	do. 4½m.; do. 3m.; do. 3½m.
525	1 m. N.E. of Sg. na Sgine (end of shoulder)	do. 4m.; do. 3¾m.; do. 3¾m.
189	2¼ m. E. from Lochhournhead	Kinlochhourn, 2¼ m.; Tomdoun Inn, 11¼ m.
459	¾ m. N.N.E. from Sgùrr a' Mhaoraich	do. 2¾ m.; do. 10½ m.
408	½ m. W. by N. do. ...	do. 1¾ m.; do. 10¾ m.
172	1¾ m. N. from Loch Quoich	G'quoich Lo., 1¾m.; Cluanie 4½m.; T'doun 7¼m.
231	⅔ m. E.S.E. from Gleouraich	do. 1⅞m.; do. 4½m.; do. 7½m.
252	1¾ m. N. from foot of Loch Quoich ...	do. 2½m.; do. 4¾m.; do. 5½m.
407	2⅝ m. S.S.E. from Cluanie Inn	Cluanie[18], 2⅝ m.
289	1 m. N.W. from Creag a' Mhàim ...	do. 2 m. S.
	Maol Chinn-dearg—	
201	2½ m. W. by N. from Creag a' Mhàim	do. 2½ m. S.W. by S.
299	1¼ m. W. by N. of Aonach air Chrith	do. 3¼ m. S.W. by W.
250	⅔ m. S.E. from Sgùrr an Lochain ...	do. 4 m. W.S.W.
239	S. side of Glen Shiel	do. 4½ m. W. by S.; Shiel Bridge[2] 6¾m.
523	1½ m. W.N.W. from Sgùrr an Lochain	do. 6¾ m.; do. 5¾m.
	SECTION 8.	
	Five Sisters, or *Beinn Mhòr Range*—	
119	N. side of Glen Shiel 3m. E.S.E. of Shiel Br.	Shiel Br.[2] 3 m.; Cluanie[18] 7 m.; Airdferry Hot.
251	⅝ m. S. from Sgùrr Fhuaran	do. 3¼ m.; do. 5½ m. [(L. Alsh), 8½ m.
186	1 m. E.S.E. do.	do. 3¾ m.; do. 6 m.
379	⅔ m. E. from Sgùrr na Ciste Duibhe ...	do. 4¼ m.; do. 5½ m.
386	1 m. W. by N. of Sgùrr a' Bhealaich Dheirg	Cluanie[18], 4¼ m.; Shiel Bridge,[2] 5¾ m.
180	N. side head of Glen Shiel	do. 3¼ m.; do. 6¾ m.
236	2¼ m. N.W. by W. from Cluanie Inn ...	do. 2¼ m.; do. 7¾ m.
276	⅓ m. E.N.E. from Aonach Meadhoin ...	do. 2 m.; do. 8 m.
293	3¼ m. N.N.W. from Cluanie Inn ...	do. 3¼ m.
81	3½ m. N.N.E. do. ...	do. 3½ m.
152	⅓ m. E.N.E. from Centre Top	do. 3¾ m.
227	¾ m. S.S.W. do. ...	do. 3 m.
55	2¼ m. N.N.E. from Cluanie Inn ...	do. 2¼ m.
468	1¼ m. E.N.E. from A' Chràlaig	do. 3¼ m.
234	Between Lochs Affric and Cluanie ...	do. 4¼ m.
242	⅓ m. N.N.E. of S.S.W. Top	do. 4½ m.
475	¾ m. do. do.	do. 5 m.
506	⅔ m. E.S.E. do.	do. 4½ m.
73	2¼ m. N. from Loch Cluanie	do. 3½ m.
223	½ m. W.S.W. of Sgùrr nan Conbhairean	do. 3 m.
261	⅝ m. S.E. do. do.	do. 3¾ m.
366	1¾ m. N. from Loch Cluanie	do. 4¼ m. E. by N.
531	3¼ m. E.N.E. of Croe Br., head of L. Duich	Shiel Br.[2] 5¼ m.; Croe Br., 3¼ m.; Airdferry Hot.
	Beinn Fhada (*Ben Attow*)—	8 [(L. Alsh), 8½m.
176	4 m. E. from head of Loch Duich ...	do. 5¼ m.; Croe Bridge, 2¾ m.; do. 10m.
354	1 m. W. by N. of Beinn Fhada, Main Top	do. 4¼ m.; do. 4 m.
411	1 m. E.S.E. do.	do. 6 m.; do. 4¾ m.
36	6½ m. E. by N. from head of Loch Duich }	Alltbeath (Glen Affric), 2¼ m.; Affric Lodge 8m.;
43	¼ m. W. from Centre Top ... }	Invercannich, 18 m.; Cluanie[18], 7 m.; Croe
353	⅔ m. E.S.E. do. ... }	Br., 6¼ m.; Shiel Br.,[2] 8 m.; Airdferry Hot.,
421	1 m. E. by S. do. ... }	12 m.
127	⅝ m. N.N.W. do. ... }	Alltbeath (Gl. Affric), 2¾ m.; Affric Lo., 8¼ m.;
270	1 m. N. by W. do. ... }	Invercannich,[16] 18¾ m.; Cluanie,[18] 7¾ m.;
238	1 m. W.N.W. do. ... }	Croe Br., 6 m.

now " Five Sisters "]. [8] [Three of the " Five Sisters of Kintail," the others being Sgùrr na Mòraich (2870) and Sgùrr nan Saighead (2950 contour)]. [9] Sgùrr nan Ceathreamhan, in 1st edn. [10] [The eastmost of two small 3250 contours]. [11] Mr Colin Phillip, in very uncertain weather. [12] Sir H. T. Munro. The only height on 6-in. map is 3014, a little to S. of the county march, apparently not on the top. [13] [Sir H. T. Munro]. [14] Prof. Heddle. [15] The name on 6-in. map is at least 1m. N.N.E. of the 3250 contour locally known by that name. [16] Glenaffric Hotel. [17] The " E. Top " of the 1st edn. [18] [Cluanie Inn is again open (1952)].

34 — Munro's Tables of the 3000-Feet Tops.

NAME. SECT. 8—Contd. HEIGHT. §	COUNTY. 1" O/S sheet No.	Sep. Mt.	Top.	Map Ref.
Creag a' Choir' Aird,* ‡ (Southern Top ²) (3150) 3210 ap.¹	Ross ... 26	167	303	08 25
Creag a' Choir' Aird,* ² (N. Top) 3188	do. ... ,,	...	328	08 26
do. (E. Top) ... (3000) 3058	do. ... ,,	...	457	08 26
An Socach * 3017	Inv., Ross ,,	266	514	09 23
Mam Sodhail (Mam Soul) 3862	do. ,,	13	23	12 25
Creag a' Chaoruinn 3462	Inverness ,,	...	136	11 23
[Stob] Coire Coulavie (W. side) (Top of . . . .) 3508	Inv., Ross ,,	...	116	11 24
Ciste Dhubh * ... ... (3600) 3606	do. ,,	...	86	11 24
An Tudair (Saoiter Mòr) ... small 3500 contour	Inverness ,,	...	123	12 24
Mullach Cadha Rainich † ³ ... ... (3250) 3262	do. ,,	...	258	14 24
Sgùrr na Làpaich 3401	do. 27	...	170	15 24
Càrn Eige ... ... (3880) 3877	Inv., Ross 26	12	20	12 26
[Stob] Coire Lochan (Top of . . . .) ... (3000) 3006	Ross ,,	...	530	12 27
Creag na h-Eige ... ... (3750) 3753	Inv., Ross ,,	...	40	13 26
[Stob] Coire Dhomhnuill‡¹⁸ (Top above . . . .)				
(3650) 3725	do. ,,	...	45	13 26
Sròn Garbh † ... ... (3650) 3705	do. ,,	...	49	14 26
Beinn Fhionnlaidh 3294	Ross ... ,,	124	230	11 28
Tom a' Chòinich 3646	Inv., Ross 27	40	67	16 27
Tom a' Chòinich Beag † ... ... (3350) 3450 ap.⁴	do. ,,	...	141	15 27
An Leth-Chreag * ... ... (3400) 3443	do. ,,	...	146	15 27
Toll Creagach (Tuill Creagach) 3452	Inverness ,,	73	140	19 28
do. W. Top (Top N. of the Allt Toll Easa)(3150) 3149	do. ,,	...	355	17 27

SECTION 9.

Càrn nan Gobhar (S. of Gl. Strath Farrar) ... 3251	Inverness 27	148	267	18 34
Creag Dubh 3102	do. ,,	...	405	20 35
Sgùrr na Làpaich 3773	Inv., Ross ,,	21	34	16 35
Rudha na Spreidhe * (. . . . Spreidha) (3400) 3484 ap.⁵	Inverness ,,	...	131	16 35
Sgùrr nan Clachan Geala * ... ... (3500) 3591 ap.⁶	Ross ... ,,	...	92	16 34
Creag a' Chaoruinn * ... ... (3050) 3195 ap.⁷	do. ,,	...	317	16 33
Bràigh a' Choire Bhig ... ... (3350) 3303	do. ,,	...	220	15 33
An Riabhachan (N.E. Top) ... ... 3696 ⁸	Inv., Ross 26	28	52	13 34
do. (W. Top) ... ... (3400) 3406 ⁹	Ross ... ,,	...	167	12 33
An Socach ... ... (3508) 3503	do. ,,	66	120	10 33
Sgùrr na Ruaidhe ¹⁰ (Sgùrr Ruadh) ... 3254	Inv., Ross 27	146	264	28 42
Càrn nan Gobhar ¹⁰ (N. of Gl. Strath Farrar) ... 3242	do. ,,	150	275	27 43
Sgùrr a' Choire Ghlais ¹⁰ 3554	do. ,,	55	100	25 43
Sgùrr Fhuar-thuill ¹⁰ 3439	do. ,,	78	150	23 43
Creag Ghorm a' Bhealaich ¹⁰ 3378	do. ,,	...	181	24 43
Sgùrr na Fearstaig ¹⁰ (Sg. na Festig) 3326	do. ,,	...	207	22 43
Creag Toll a' Choin ... ... (3250) 3295	Ross ... 26	123	228	13 45
Maoile Lunndaidh (Maoile Lunndaich) ... 3294	do. ,,	...	229	13 45
Càrn nam Fiaclan 3253	do. ,,	...	266	12 45
Sgùrr a' Chaorachain (Sg. a' Chaoruinn) (3455) 3452	do. ,,	72	139	08 44
Bidean an Eòin Deirg 3430	do. ,,	...	154	10 44
Sgùrr Choinnich 3260	do. ,,	143	260	07 44
Bidein a' Choire Sheasgaich 3102	do. ,,	214	406	04 41
Lurg Mhòr 3234	do. ,,	154	283	06 40
Meall Mòr ¹² 3190	do. ,,	...	325	07 40
Moruisg ... ... (3026) 3033	do. ,,	259	494	10 50

SECTION 10.

Maol Chean-dearg (Meall a' Chinn Deirg) ... 3060	Ross ... ,,	235	449	92 50
Sgòrr Ruadh (Sgùrr Ruadh) 3142	do. ,,	192	364	96 50
Beinn Liath Mhòr 3034	do. ,,	258	493	96 52
Beinn Alligin—				
Sgùrr Mhòr (Sgùrr Mòr) 3232	do. ... ,,	155	285	86 61
Tom na Gruagaich (Spidean Coir' an Laoigh)	do. ... ,,	...	507	85 60
Liathach— (3024) 3021				
Spidean a' Choire Lèith 3456	do. ,,	71	138	93 58
Mullach an Rathain 3358	do. ,,	...	193	91 57
Bidean Toll a' Mhuic † ... ... (2850) 3200 ap.¹³	do. ,,	...	312	93 58
Stùc a' Choire Dhuibh Bhig ... (2800) 3050 ap.¹⁴	do. ,,	...	470	94 58
Meall Dearg † ... ... (2850) 3150 ap.¹⁵	do. ,,	...	352	91 58
Am Fasarinen* (Spideanan nam Fasarinen) (2850) 3050 ap.¹⁵	do. ,,	...	463	92 57

* Named only on the 6-inch map.   † Local name, not given on either O.S. map.
‡ New top, not in the original Tables.   § The 1-in. height is given in parenthesis if different from 6-in.

¹ [Sir H. T. Munro and Rev. A. E. Robertson].   ² A 3000-ft. contour on the 1-in. map extends 2½m.
nearly N. and S., with an apparent width of under ¼ mile.   The N.W. end is Creag a' Choire Aird.
No height or name is given to the S. portion of the ridge, but from the shaded 1-in. map it appears at
least higher than Creag a'Choire Aird. Dr Corner's measurements along the ridge—Tops 1m., 1½m.,
and 1¾m. from the E. peak of Ceathreamhnan, 3060, 3080, and 3075 respectively.   ³ [Mr R. Burn:
in 1st edn., " Top between Mam Sodhail and Sgurr na Lapaich "].   ⁴ Prof. Heddle.   ⁵ [Dr Corner].
⁶ [Dr Corner].   ⁷ [Dr Corner].   ⁸ [This is the correct height, the hill-shading, on which

Top No.	Position. **SECT. 8**—*Contd.*	Best Ascended From
303	½ m. S. of Creag a' Choir' Aird, N. Top	Shiel Br.,[17] 10¼ m.; Croe Bridge, 8¼m.; Cluanie,[20] 9¼ m.
328	2¾ m. N.E. by N. of Sg. Ceathreamhnan	
457	⅓ m.E.N.E. of Creaga' Choir' Aird, N. Top	
514	2 m. E. of Sg. Ceathreamhnan, Centre Top	Alltbeath, 1¾m.; Cluanie,[20] 7m.; Shiel Br.,[17] 10m.
23	2½ m. N.W. from Loch Affric	Alltbeath (Gl. Affric), 4 m.; Shiel Bridge,[17] 12 m.; Affric Lo., 4½ m.; Cluanie,[20] 9 m.; Invercannich,[16] 14¼ m.
136	1½ m. S. by W. from Mam Sodhail	
116	1 m. S.W. do.	
86	½ m. S.W. do.	
123	1 m. S.E. by S. do.	
258	1¼ m. E. by S. do.	
170	2¼ m. E. by S. do.	
20	½ m. N.N.E. from Mam Sodhail	Alltbeath (Gl. Affric), 4¾ m.; Affric Lo., 4¼ m.; Cluanie,[20] 9½ m.; Shiel Br.,[17] 12½ m.; Invercannich,[16] 14 m.
530	⅔ m. N.N.W. from Càrn Eige ...	
40	½ m. E.N.E. do.	
45	⅞ m. E. do.	
49	1¼ m. E. do.	
230	1⅓ m. N.N.W. do.	As Càrn Eige.
67	2¾ m. E.N.E. from Càrn Eige	Affric Lo., 3 m.; Invercannich,[16] 11¼ m.
141	Small Top ⅓ m. W. of Tom a' Chòinich	do. 3¼ m.; do. 11¾ m.
146	¾ m. W.S.W. from do. ...	do. 3¼ m.; do. 12 m.
140	1½ m. S. from Loch Mullardoch ...	do. 3¼ m.; do. 9¼ m.
355	1⅛ m. W.S.W. from Toll Creagach ...	do. 3 m.; do. 10½ m.
	SECTION 9.	
267	2¼ m. N. of Loch Mullardoch ...	Monar Lo., 3¾ m.; Invercannich, 9¾ m.
405	1¼ m. E.N.E. of Càrn nan Gobhar	
34	2¾ m. N. from Loch Mullardoch ...	Monar Lo., 4 m.; Invercannich,[16] 11¼ m.
131	¼ m. N. by E. from Sgùrr na Làpaich ...	do. 3¾ m.; do. 11¼ m.
92	⅝ m. S. by E. do. ...	do. 4¼ m.; do. 11 m.
317	1 m. S.S.E. do. ...	do. 4½ m.; do. 10¾ m.
220	1⅛ m. S. by W. do. ...	do. 5 m.; do. 11¼ m.
52	Between Lochs Lungard and Monar ...	do. 5 m.; do. 12½ m.
167	1½ m. W.S.W. of N.E. Top	do. 6½ m.; do. 13¾ m.
120	1 m. W.S.W. of 3406 Top of Riabhachan	Shiel Br.,[17] 14½ m.; do. 14½ m.
264	2½ m. N.N.W. of L. Beannacharan [11]	Corrysleuch (Gl. Orrin), 2¾ m.; Struy Br., 7¼ m Mulie, 2¾ m.; Inv'c'ich,[16] 7 m. [Inv'c'ich 8½m.
275	1 m. E.N.E. of Sgùrr a' Choire Ghlais	
100	3 m. N.W. by N. from Loch a' Mhuilidh [11]	Mulie,[11] 3¼ m.; Struy Br., 9 m.; Monar Lo., 4 m.
150	1½m. W.N.W. from Sgùrr a' Choire Gnlais	do. 4½ m.; do. 10¾ m.; do. 3¼ m.; Invercannich, 9¼ m.
181	⅝ m. E.S.E. of Sgùrr Fhuar-thuill	
207	½ m. W. do.	
228	2¾ m. N. from head of Loch Monar	Strathmore Lo. (L. Monar), 2¾ m.; Glencarron Sta., 5½ m.; Achnasheen, 8½ m.
229	½ m. N.E. from Creag Toll a' Choin	
266	½ m. W. by N. do.	
139	3¼ m. N.W. from head of Loch Monar	Strathmore Lo., 3¼ m.; Glencarron Sta., 4 m.; Achnasheen, 9¾ m.
154	1 m. E. by S. of Sg. a' Chaorachain	
260	¾ m. W. do.	
406	4¾ m. W. from head of Loch Monar ...	Strathmore Lo., 4¾ m.; Strathcarron Hot., 6¾ m.
283	3½ m. W. do. ...	do. 3¾ m.; do. 7¾ m.
325	½ m. E. by N. from Lurg Mhòr ...	do. 3¼ m.; do. 8¼ m.
494	2½ m. E. from Glencarron Station ...	Glencarron Station, 2½ m.; Achnasheen, 6¼ m.
	SECTION 10.	
449	5 m. N. from head of Loch Carron ...	St'carron Inn, 6m.; Torridon, 4m.; Kin'ewe 10m.
364	3 m. W.N.W. of Achnashellach Station	do. 5¼m.; do. 4¾m.; do. 8¼m.
493	1 m. N. by E. from Sgòrr Ruadh ...	do. 6¼m.; do. 4½m.; do. 7¼m.; [Achnashellach Sta., 3 m.
	Beinn Alligin—	
284	4 m. N.W. from Torridon	Torridon, 3½ m.; Kinlochewe Hotel, 10 m.
507	¾ m. S.S.W. from Sgùrr Mhòr ...	do. 3¼ m.; do. 10½ m.
	Liathach—[19]	
138	2¼ m. E.N.E. from Torridon	Torridon, 2¼ m.; Kinlochewe Hotel, 6½ m.
193	1 m. W. by S. of Sp. a' Choire Lèith	do. 1¼ m. N.E.; do. 7½ m.
312	⅓ m. E.N.E. do. ...	do. 2¾ m.; do. 6¼ m.
470	⅝ m. E. by N. do. ...	do. 3 m.; do. 6 m.
352	¼ m. N.N.E. of Mullach an Rathain ...	do. 1½ m.; do. 7¼ m.
463	½ m. E. do. ...	do. 1½ m.; do. 7¼ m.

the 3730 estimate of last edition was based, having been found erroneous, and the 3700 confirming contour now stated to be only approximate. The county boundary top is not more than 10 ft. lower, there being a point 3686 close to the boundary]. [9] The point on the main ridge marked 3559 on both the 6-in. and 1-in. maps, is only a portion of the ridge of the main E. summit, the real W. top being ⅓m. W. by N. from this point, and 3406 high. [10] Best ascended from Struy Bridge. [11] In Glen Strath Farrar. [12] The name on both 6-in. and 1-in. maps is about 1m. E. of the top. [13] Prof. Norman Collie. [14] [Sir H. T. Munro]. [15] Prof. Norman Collie. [16] Glenaffric Hotel. [17] [Shiel Inn is now closed]. [18] (*Dhomhain, new 1-in. map*). [19] Positions of "ap." tops approximate. [20] [Cluanie Inn is again open (1952)].

NAME. SECT. 10—*Contd.*	HEIGHT.§	COUNTY. 1″ O/S sheet No.	No. in order of Alt. Sep. Mt.	Top.	Map Ref.
Beinn Eighe (Ben Eay) Range—					
Ruadh-stac-Mòr	3309	Ross 26	116	215	95 61
Sàil Mhòr	3217	do. ,,	...	296	93 60
A' Choinneach Mhòr* (*Còinneach Mhòr*) (3000)	3130 [1]	do. ,,	...	376	95 60
Spidean Coire nan Clach † ... (3000)	3220 ap.[2]	do. ,,	...	290	96 59
Sgùrr Bàn	3188	do. ,,	...	329	97 59
Sgùrr an Fhir Duibhe † ... ... (3150)	3160	do. ,,	...	347	98 60
Creag Dubh † ... ... (3000)	3050 ap.[3]	do. ,,	...	466	98 60
SECTION 11.					
Slioch ... ... [5](3250)	3217 [4]	Ross 19 20	161	294	00 69
Sgùrr an Tuill Bhàin	3058	do. ,, ,,	...	455	01 68
A' Mhaighdean ... ... (2850)	3060 ap.[6]	do. ,, ,,	237	451	00 75
Beinn Tarsuinn	3080 ap.[29]	do. ,, ,,	...	...	03 72
Mullach Coire Mhic Fhearchair ... **(3326)**	3327 [7]	do. ,, ,,	112	206	05 73
Sgùrr Bàn ... ... **(3200)**	3194 [8]	do. ,, ,,	176	319	05 74
An Teallach Range— [27]					
Bidein a' Ghlas Thuill	3483	Ross ,, ,,	69	132	06 84
Glas Mheall Mòr ... ... (3100)	3176	do. ,, ,,	...	337	07 85
Glas Mheall Liath * ... (3150)	3080 ap.[9]	do. ,, ,,	...	433	07 84
Sgùrr Fiòna	3474	do. ,, ,,	...	134	06 83
Sgùrr Creag an Eich * ... (3300)	3350 ap.[10]	do. ,, ,,	...	196	05 83
Lord Berkeley's Seat † ... (3250)	3380 ap.[11]	do. ,, ,,	...	179	06 83
Corrag Bhuidhe * ... ... (3250)	3360 ap.[12]	do. ,, ,,	...	192	06 83
Corrag Bhuidhe Buttress † ‡ ... (3100)	3050 ap.[13]	do. ,, ,,	...	465	06 83
[Stob] Cadha Gobhlach† (*Top above*) (3150)	3040 ap.[14]	do. ,, ,,	...	483	06 82
Sàil Liath ‡ ... ... (3150)	3100 ap.[15]	do. 19 20	...	412	07 82
Fannaich District—					
A' Chailleach	3276	Ross 20	133	243	13 71
Sgùrr Breac ... ... (3100)	3240 ap.[16]	do. ,,	151	278	15 71
Meall a' Chrasgaidh	3062	do. ,,	234	448	18 73
Sgùrr nan Clach Geala	3581	do. ,,	51	93	18 71
Sgùrr nan Each	3026	do. ,,	262	503	18 69
Sgùrr Mòr	3637	do. ,,	41	71	20 71
Càrn na Criche ... ... (3000)	3148	do. ,,	...	358	19 72
Meall nam Peithirean * ... (3100)	3130 ap.[17]	do. ,,	...	378	20 70
Beinn Liath Mhòr Fannaich ... (3000)	3120 ap.[18]	do. ,,	206	391	22 72
Meall Gorm, N.W. Top (*Meallan Rairigidh*)	3109	do. ,,	208	395	22 69
do. S.E. Top ... ... (3000)	3030 ap.[19]	do. ,,	...	498	23 69
An Coileachan	3015	do. ,,	269	517	24 68
Fionn Bheinn	3059	do. 26	236	450	14 62
SECTION 12.					
Ben Wyvis—					
Glas Leathad Mòr (Main Top)[28] ...	3429	Ross 21	82	157	46 68
An Cabar	3106	do. ,,	...	399	45 66
Tom a' Chòinnich	3134	do. ,,	...	373	46 70
Glas Leathad Beag * (Centre Top)[20] (3000)	3077 ap.[20]	do. ,,	...	437	49 70
Glas Leathad Beag * (W. Top) ... (3000)	3027 ap.[21]	do. ,,	...	502	48 70
Fiachlach (E. Top) [22] (*Feachdach*) ...	3018	do. ,,	...	513	49 71
Am Faochagach (*Am Fraochagach*)	3120	do. 20	204	388	30 79
Cona' Mheall ... ... (3150)	3200 ap.[23]	do. ,,	170	307	27 81
Beinn Dearg	3547	do. ,,	58	106	25 81
Meall nan Ceapràichean ... ... (3150)	3192 ap.[24]	do. ,,	179	323	26 82
Ceann Garbh * ... ... (3050)	3063	do. ,,	...	447	26 83
Eididh nan Clach Geala	3039	do. ,,	253	486	25 84
Seana Bhraigh ... ... (3040)	3041	do. ,,	251	481	28 87
SECTION 13.					
Ben More, Assynt	3273	Sutherland 13	136	247	32 20
do. (South Top) ... ... (3100)	3200 ap.[25]	do. ,,	...	309	32 19
Cona-mheall (Conival)	3234	do. ,,	153	282	30 20
Ben Klibreck (*Ben Clibrig*) [26]	3154	do. 14	188	350	58 29
Ben Hope	3040	do. 9	252	484	47 50

* *Named only on the 6-inch map.*   † *Local name, not given on either O.S. map.*
‡ *New top, not in the original Tables.*   § *The 1-in. height is given in parenthesis if different from 6-in*

[1] The top lies W. from the 3130 point, and is somewhat higher: the name on 6-in. map is ⅜m. to the
S.E. of the 3130 point.   [2] Prof. Heddle and Mr Colin Phillip: certainly higher than Sgùrr Bàn and
Sgùrr an Fhir Duibhe.   [3] [Estimate from hill-shaded 1-in. map.]   [4] [See 'Additional Notes '; in first
and successive editions 3260 ft., from entry in a visitors' book at Kinlochewe by Capt. Kirkwood,R.E.]
[5] 200 yds. E.S.E. of the 3217 ft. point on the 6-in. and 1-in. maps. [but see 'Additional Notes ']
[6] [Sir H. T. Munro]: over 3100 ft., Mr Colin Phillip and Prof. Heddle, in 1st edition of the Tables

Top No.	Position. SECT. 10—*Contd.*	Best Ascended From
	Beinn Eighe Range (S. of L. Maree)—	
215	N.W. spur of Beinn Eighe	Kinlochewe Hotel, 4¾ m.
296	W. end of do.	do. 5½ m.; L. Maree Hotel 6¼m.
376	⅝ m. S. of Ruadh-stac Mòr	do. 5 m.
290	⅝ m. W.S.W. from Sgùrr Bàn ...	do. 4 m.
329	3½ m. S.W. from head of Loch Maree	do. 3½ m.
347	½ m. E. from Sgùrr Bàn	do. 3 m.
466	⅞ m. N.E. do.	do. 2¾ m.
	SECTION 11.	
294	1½ m. N. from E. end of Loch Maree ...	Kinlochewe Hotel, 4½ m.
455	¾ m. S.S.E. from Slioch	do. 4¼ m.
451	3¾ m. N. do.	do. 8¼ m.; L. Maree Hot., 6¼ m.
...	1 m. S.W. of Mull. Co. Mhic Fhearchair	do. 6¾ m.
206	4 m. N.E. from Slioch	do. 7¼ m. [(by boat).
319	¾ m. N. of Mullach Coire Mhic Fhearchair	do. 8 m.
	An Teallach Range—[27]	
132	2¾ m. S.S.W. from Dundonnell ...	Dundonnell (Little Loch Broom), 2¾ m.
337	¾ m. N.E. of Bidein a' Ghlas Thuill	do. do. 2 m.
433	½ m. E. by S. do. ...	do. do. 2⅜ m.
134	½ m. S.W. by W. do. ...	do. do. 3¼ m.
196	½ m. W. from Sgùrr Fiòna	do. do. 3½ m.
179	200 yards S. do.	do. do. 3⅓ m.
192	¼ m. S. do.	do. do. 3⅓ m.
465	⅓m. S.S.E. from Corrag Bhuidhe ...	do. do. 3½ m.
483	½ m. S.S.E. do. ...	do. do. 3½ m.
412	S.E. end of An Teallach Range ...	do. do. 3¾ m.
	Fannaich District—	
243	3 m. N.W. by N. of W. end L. Fannich }	Braemore Lodge, 6¼ m.; Fannich Lodge, 6¼ m.;
278	1⅓ m. E. from A' Chailleach ... }	Kinlochewe, 9 m.; Achnasheen, 8¼ m.
448	3¾m. S. by W. of Braemore Lodge ...	B'more Lo, 3¾m.; F'nich Lo, 5m.; Ach'shn 9¼m.
93	2¾m. N.N.E. from W. end of L. Fannich	do. 5m.; Fannich Lo, 4m.; Ach'sheen, 8¼m.
503	1 m. S. from Sgùrr nan Clach Geala	Fan'h Lo, 3¼m; Ach'sheen, 7¼m; Ach'nalt, 7¼m.
71	3¾ m. N.N.W. from Fannich Lodge	do. 3¾m.; Aultguish Inn, 9¼m.; Achanalt 7¼m.
358	⅔ m. N.W. from Sgùrr Mòr	do. 4¼m.; do. 9¾m.; do. 8m.
378	¾ m. S.S.E. do.	do. 3m.; do. 9m.; do. 6¾ m.
391	1 m. E.N.E. do.	do. 4m.; do. 8¼m.; do. 7¼ m.
395	2¼ m. N. from Fannich Lodge ...	do. 2¼m.; do. 8½m.; do. 6½m.
498	⅔ m. E.S.E. from Meall Gorm ...	do. 2¼m.; do. 7½m.; do. 5¼m.
517	2 m. N.E. from Fannich Lodge ...	do. 2m.; do. 7m.; do. 4¼m.
450	2½ m. N.N.W. from Achnasheen ...	Ach'sheen, 2½m.; Kinl'ewe, 7½m.; Ach'alt, 7m.
	SECTION 12.	
	Ben Wyvis Range—	
157	6½ m. N. by W. from Strathpeffer ...	Strathpeffer, 6½m.; Garve, 6m.; Evanton, 9¼m.
399	1⅓ m. S.W. by S. from Main Top ...	do. 5¾m.; do. 4¾m.; do. 9¾m.
373	1 m. N. from do. ...	do. 7½m.; do. 7m.; do. 9¼m.
437	2⅓ m. N.E. do. ...	do. 8m.; Evanton, 7¾ m.
502	2 m. N.E. do. ...	do. 7¾m.; do. 8 m.
513	2¾ m. N.E. do.	do. 8¼m.; do. 7½m.
388	Strathvaich, 3 m. E.S.E. of Beinn Dearg	Aultguish Inn, 6¼ m.
307	do. 1 m. E. by N. do. }	Braemore Lodge, 4¾ m.; Aultguish Inn, 8½ m.;
106	5½ m. S.E. of Inverlael, head of L. Broom }	Inverlael, 6¼ m.; Ullapool, 11¼ m.
323	¾ m. N. of Beinn Dearg	Inverlael, 5m.; Aultguish, 9½m.; Ullapool, 10¾m.
447	¾ m. N.E. of Meall nan Ceapràichean ...	do. 5½m.; do. 9½m.; do. 10¾m.
486	4¾ m. E. by S. of Inverlael, L. Broom ...	do. 6½m.; Ullapool, 10 m.
481	6 m. E. by N. do. ...	do. 6½ m.; do. 10 m.
	SECTION 13.	
247	4¼ m. E. by S. of Inchnadamph, L. Assynt	Inchnadamph, 4¼ m.
309	⅝ m. S.E. from North Top	do. 4¾ m.
282	3½ m. E. by S. from Inchnadamph ...	do. 3½ m.
350	3⅓ m. S. by E. of Altnaharra Inn, L. Naver	Altnaharra Inn, 3½ m.
484	1½ m. E. of the south end of Loch Hope	Cashel Dhu (shepherd's) 1¾m; Eriboll (no I.) 5m.

[7] 1st edn., 3320 ft. Mr Colin Phillip. [8] [By the hill-shaded 1-in. map the actual top is about ⅕m, S.W. of the 3194 point]. [9] Prof. Heddle. [10] Prof. Heddle. [11] Sir H. T. Munro's estimate: 1st edn., 3300, Mr Colin Phillip. [12] Prof. Heddle. [13] Sir H. T. Munro. [14] Prof. Heddle. At the N.W. end of the ridge of which Sàil Liath is at the S.E. end. [15] Sir H. T. Munro. [16] Mr Colin Phillip. [17] [Sir H. T. Munro]. [18] [Sir H. T. Munro]. [19] [Dr Corner]. [20] [Dr Corner; "almost a separate mt." H.T.M.; in 1st edn., "Top of Coire Lochain"]. [21] [Dr Corner]. [22] The name on 6-in. and 1-in. maps is ⅝m. N. of the top. [23] Mr Colin Phillip's estimate; levels taken from Beinn Dearg. [24] [Mr R. Burn]. [25] Prof. Heddle's estimate. [26] On 6-in. map the 3154 point is named Meall nan Eòin, and on the 1-in. map Meall nan Con. [27] Positions of 'ap.' tops approximate. [28] ['Glas Leathad Mòr', in the new 1-in. map, apparently refers to the lower slopes of the whole ridge, not the top]. [29] [See 'Additional Notes', p. 42].

NAME.	HEIGHT.§	COUNTY. 1" O/S sheet No.	No. in order of Alt. Sep. Mt.	Top.	Map Ref.

SECTION 14.

NAME.	HEIGHT.§	COUNTY. 1" O/S sheet No.	Sep. Mt.	Top.	Map Ref.
Ben Avon, Eastern Cairngorms—					
Leabaidh an Daimh Bhuidhe[1] (Main or Cen. Top)3843		Ab'n, B'nff 38 41	15	27	13 01
S.W. Top ... ... (3700) 3729		do. ,, ,,	...	44	12 01
East Meur Gorm Craig ... ... (3000) 3075		Banff ... ,, ,,	...	438	16 04
West * do. 3354		do. ,, ,,	...	194	15 03
Stob Bac an Fhurain* (*Stob Dubh, Bruach an* ...) 3533		do. ,, ,,	...	111	13 03
Mullach Lochan nan Gabhar ... (3655) 3662		Ab'n, B'nff ,, ,,	...	58	14 02
Stùc Gharbh Mhòr [2] 3625		do. ,, ,,	...	78	14 01
Stob Dubh an Eàs Bhig ... (3400) 3563 ap.[3]		Aberdeen ,, ,,	...	98	13 00
Càrn Eàs 3556		do. ,, ,,	...	99	12 99
Creag an Dail Mhòr * (*Cr. na Dàla Moire*) 3189		do. ,, ,,	...	327	13 98
Beinn a' Bhàird, Eastern Cairngorms—					
North Top 3924		Ab'n, B'nff ,, ,,	10	18	09 00
South Top 3860		Aberdeen ,, ,,	...	24	09 98
Cnap a' Chleirich 3811		Ab'n, B'nff ,, ,,	...	30	10 00
Stob an t-Sluichd 3621		Banff ,, ,,	...	79	11 02
A' Chioch ‡ ... ... 3500 contour		Aberdeen ,, ,,	...	122	09 98
Beinn Bhreac (East Top) 3051		do. ,, ,, 243		462	05 97
do. (West Top) ... (3000) 3045 ap.[4]		do. ,, ,,	...	477	05 97
Beinn a' Chaorruinn 3553		Ab'n, B'nff ,, ,,	56	101	04 01
Beinn a' Chaorruinn Bheag * 3326		do. ,, ,,	...	208	05 01
Bynack More [5] (*Caiplich, Ben Bynac*) ... 3574		Inverness ,, ,,	52	95	04 06
A' Chòinneach * 3345		B'nff, Inv. ,, ,,	105	198	03 04
Beinn Mheadhoin (N.E. Top) 3883		Banff ... ,, ,,	11	19	02 01
do. (S.W. Top) 3750		Ab'n, B'nff ,, ,,	...	41	01 01
[Stob] Coire Etchachan (*Top N. of ...* .) 3551		do. ,, ,,	...	103	02 00
Stacan Dubha * ‡ ... ... (3200) 3330 ap.[6]		Banff ,, ,,	...	205	01 01
Derry Cairngorm 3788		Aberdeen ,, ,,	19	32	01 98
Sgùrr an Lochan Uaine * ‡ ... (3150) 3220 ap.[7]		do. ,, ,,	...	291	02 99
Little Cairngorm † ‡ ... ... (3350) 3450 ap.[8]		do. ,, ,,	...	142	02 97
Càrn a' Mhaim ... ... (3329) 3400 ap.[9]		do. ,, ,,	91	171	99 95
Ben Macdui (Macdhui) (Main Top) ... 4300		Ab'n, B'nff ,, ,,	2	2	98 99
do. (North Top) ... 4244		do. ,, ,,	...	4	99 99
[Stob] Coire Sputan Dearg [10] ... (4050) 4095		Aberdeen ,, ,,	...	7	99 98
Creagan a' Choire Etchachan ... 3629		do. ,, ,,	...	76	01 99
Sròn Riach * ... ... (3600) 3534		do. ,, ,,	...	110	99 97
Cairn Etchachan * (*Top of cliffs above L. Avon*) 3673		Ab'n, B'nff ,, ,,	...	56	00 01
Cairn Gorm 4084		B'nff, Inv. ,, ,,	5	9	00 04
Cairn Lochan (*Top of Coire an Lochain*) ... 3983		do. ,, ,,	...	16	98 02
Fiacaill Coire an t-Sneachda * ... (3500) 3640 ap.[11]		Inverness ,, ,,	...	70	99 03
[Stob] Coire an t-Sneachda (*Top of ...*) (3850) 3856		B'nff, Inv. ,, ,,	...	26	99 03
Fiacaill a' Choire Chais ... ... (3700) 3737		do. ,, ,,	...	42	00 04
Cnap Coire na Spreidhe 3772		Inverness ,, ,,	...	35	01 05
Sròn a' Cha-no * ... ... (3300) 3388 ap.[12]		do. ,, ,,	...	174	01 06
Creag an Leth-choin (Sth. Top) (*Cr. na Leacainn*) 3448		do. ,, ,,	...	143	96 03
do. (North Top) 3365		do. ,, ,,	...	188	96 04
Fiacaill na Leth-choin † ‡ ... (3500) 3550 ap.[7]		do. ,, ,,	...	104	97 03
Braeriach 4248		Ab'n, Inv.37 38 41	3	3	95 00
do. [Stob] Coire an Lochain[15] (*Top above Loch* ..) 4036		do. 37	...	11	94 99
do. South Plateau [15] ... ... 4149 [13]		do. ,,	...	6	93 98
Sròn na Lairig 3875		do. 38 41	...	21	96 01
[Stob] Lochan nan Cnapan (*Top above* ..) (3000) 3009		Inverness 37	...	526	92 95
Cairn Toul 4241		Aberdeen 38 41	4	5	96 97
[Stob] Coire an t-Saighdeir (*Top of ...*.) (3950) 3989		do. ,, ,,	...	14	96 96
Sgòr an Lochan Uaine* (The Angels' Peak) (4150) 4095 ap.[14]		do. ,, ,,	...	8	95 97
The Devil's Point 3303		do. ,, ,,	120	219	97 95
Beinn Bhrotain 3795		do. ,, ,,	18	31	95 92
Càrn Cloich-mhuillin (*C. Clioch* .. . .) 3087		do. ,, ,,	222	423	96 90
Monadh Mòr 3651		Ab'n, Inv. 37	38	65	93 94
Mullach Clach a' Bhlàir (*Meall Tionail*) 3338		Inverness ,,	110	203	88 92
Diollaid Coire Eindart * 3184		do. ,,	...	332	90 92
Meall Dubhag (*M. Dubh-achaidh*) ... 3268		do. ,,	140	253	88 95
Càrn Bàn Mòr 3443		do. ,,	75	145	89 97
Sgòr Gaoith [16] (*Sgoran Dubh, South*) ... 3658		do. ,,	36	62	90 99
Sgòran Dubh Mòr (*Sgòran Dubh, North*) 3635		do. ,,	...	74	90 00
Meall Buidhe † 3185		do. ,,	...	331	89 00
Geal Chàrn 3019		do. ,,	265	511	88 01

* *Named only on the 6-inch map.*   † *Local name, not given on either O.S. map.*
‡ *New top, not in the original Tables.*   § *The 1-in. height is given in parenthesis if different from 6-in.*

---

[1] 1st edn., " Ben Avon."   [2] Name ½m. to S. of top, on 1-in. map.   [3] Prof. Heddle.   [4] [Sir H. T. Munro; locally called Craig Derry.   The name on 1-in. map is ¾m. to N.W.].   [5] [The 3296 point, named Barns of Bynack on 1-in. map, is merely a shoulder].   [6] [Sir H. T. Munro].   [7] [Sir H. T. Munro].   [8] [Mr Colin Phillip].   [9] [The actual top is ½m. N.W. from O.S. cairn; the only height given

Top No.	Position.	Best Ascended From
	SECTION 14.	
	Ben Avon, Eastern Cairngorms—	
27	6¾ m. N. by W. from Braemar ...	Braemar, 6¾ m.; Inchrory, 5½ m.
44	Shoulder ⅝ m. S.W. from Main Top	do. 6½ m.
438	2¼ m. N.E. by E. do.	do. 7¾ m.; Inchrory, 2¾ m.; Tom't'l, 9¼m.
194	1¾ m. N.E. do.	do. 7½ m.; do. 3¼ m.; do. 9½m.
111	⅞ m. N. by E. do.	do. 7½ m.; do. 4½ m.
58	¾ m. E.N.E. do.	do. 6½ m.; do. 4¼ m.
78	⅞ m. E. by S. do. on the county march	do. 6½ m.; do. 4¾ m.
98	1 m. S. from Main Top	do. 5¾ m.; do. 5¼ m.
99	5¼ m. N.N.W. from Braemar ...	do. 5¼ m.
327	¾ m. S.E. from Càrn Eàs	do. 4½ m.
	Beinn a' Bhuird, Eastern Cairngorms—	
18	6¾ m. N.W. by N. from Braemar ...	Braemar, 6¾ m.; Inchrory, 5¼ m.
24	1¾ m. S. from North Top	do. 5½ m.
30	1 m. E.N.E. do.	do. 6½ m.; Inchrory, 5¼ m.
79	1⅞ m. N.E. do.	do. 7½ m.; do. 7¼ m.
122	½ m. N.E. of Beinn a' Bhùird, S. Top	do. 5¾ m.
462	East side of Glen Derry	Derry Lodge, 2½ m.; Braemar, 6¾ m.
477	½ m. W.N.W. from East Top	do. 2½ m.; do. 7¼ m.
101	Bet. Glens Derry and Avon, above the Learg an Laoigh.	Derry Lodge, 5 m.; Braemar, 9 m.
208	¾ m. E.N.E. of Beinn a' Chaorruinn ...	do. 5¼ m.; do. 8¾ m.
95	2¾ m. N.E. from Cairn Gorm	Nethy B., 9¼ m.; Aviem'e, 10 m.; Derry Lo., 7¼m.
198	1 m. N.N.E. from foot of Loch Avon ...	do. 10 m.; do. 9¾ m.; do. 7¼m.
19	¾ m. S.E. from Loch Avon	Derry Lo., 5¼m.; Braemar, 10 m.; Aviem'e, 10½m.
41	⅝ m. S.W. from N.E. Top	do. 5 m.; do. 8¾ m.; do. 10½m.
103	¾ m. E. from Loch Etchachan	do. 4½ m.; do. 10¾ m.; do. 11m.
205	¾ m. W. from N.E. Top	do. 5½ m.; do. 10½ m.; do. 9¾m.
32	3¼ m. N.N.W. from Derry Lodge ...	do. 3¼ m.; do. 9¼ m.
291	⅝ m. N.E. by N. from Derry Cairngorm	do. 3¾ m.; do. 9 m.
142	⅝ m. S. by E. do. ...	do. 3¾ m.; do. 8¾ m.
171	2½ m. S. by W. from Main Top B. Macdhui	do. 3¾ m.; do. 9¾ m.
2	Between Glen Derry and Glen Dee }	Derry Lodge, 4¾ m.; Aviemore, 10 m.; Nethy
4	⅜ m. N.N.E. from Main Top ... }	Bridge, 13¼ m.; Braemar, 11 m.
7	⅔ m. E.S.E. do.	Derry Lodge, 4¼ m.; Braemar, 10½ m.; Aviem'e,
76	⅜ m. S.E. from Loch Etchachan ...	do. 4¼ m.; do. 10 m. [11¼ m.
110	1 m. S.E. from Main Top	do. 3¾ m.; do. 10¼ m.
56	1½ m. N.E. by N. do.	do. 5¼ m.; do. 10¾ m.
9	1 m. N.W. from Loch Avon	Aviemore, 8½ m.; Derry Lo., 7 m.; B'mar, 8½m.
16	1½ m. S.W. by W. from Cairn Gorm ...	do. 8¼ m.; do. 6¾ m.; do. 8¼m.
70	1⅛ m. W.S.W. do. ...	do. 8 m.; do. 7 m.; do. 8m.
26	⅞ m. S.W do. ...	do. 8½ m.; do. 6½ m.; do. 8m.
42	⅓ m. W. do. ...	do. 8¼ m.; do. 7 m.; do. 8¼m.
35	¾ m. N.E. do.	do. 8½ m.; do. 7½ m.; do. 8¾m.
174	1 m.[14] N. from Cnap Coire na Spreidhe ...	do. 8½ m.; do. 8¼ m.
143	2½m. W. by S. of C'n Gorm, above Larig	do. 7¼ m.; do. 7¾ m.
188	⅜ m. N. from South Top ... [Ghru	do. 7 m.; do. 8 m.
104	⅔ m. W.N.W. from Cairn Lochan ...	do. 7¾ m.; do. 7 m.
3	2¼ m. W. by N. from Ben Macdhui ...	do. 8½ m.; do. 6¾ m.; do. 13¼m.
11	¾ m. W. by S. from Main Top	do. 8¼ m.; do. 7½ m.; do. 14m.
6	1½ m. S.W. do.	do. 9¼ m.; do. 7¼ m.; do. 13¾m.
21	⅞ m. N.E. by E. do.	do. 8½ m.; do. 6¾ m.; do. 13m.
526	1¾ m. S. from head of Loch Einich ...	do. 10¼ m.; Linn o' Dee 9¾ m.; do. 14½m.
5	West side of Glen Dee	Derry Lo. 5½ m.; B'mar, 12 m.; Aviemore 10¼m.
14	½ m. S. from Cairn Toul	do. 5¼ m.; do. 12 m.; do. 10¾m.
8	½ m. N.W. by W. from Cairn Toul ...	do. 6 m.; do. 12¾ m.; do. 9¾m.
219	1½ m. S.E. by S. do. ...	do. 4¼ m.; do. 11 m.
31	3 m. S. by W. do. ...	Linn of Dee, 7 m.; Braemar, 12 m.
423	1⅓ m. S.E. from Beinn Bhrotain ...	do. 6 m.; do. 11¼ m.
65	2½ m. S.W. by S. from Cairn Toul ...	do. 8½ m.; do. 13 m.
203	3¾ m. S.S.W. from head of Loch Einich	Kincraig Station, 8¾ m.; Hotel on main road.
332	1⅜ m. E. from Mullach Clach a' Bhlair ...	do. 9¼ m.
253	2½ m. S.W. from head of Loch Einich ...	do. 7 m.; Aviem'e, 10½ m.
145	1¼ m. W.S.W. do. ...	do. 6½ m.; do. 9½ m.
62	West side of Loch Einich	do. 6 m.; do. 8½ m.
74	⅞ m. N. from Sgòr Gaoith	do. 5½ m.; do. 7½ m.
331	¾ m. W. by S. from Sgòran Dubh Mòr ...	do. 5 m.; do. 7½ m.
511	1½ m. W.N.W. do. ...	do. 4¼ m.; do. 6¾ m.

on 6-in. map is 3329]. [10] Top of Coire an Sput Dheirg, 1st edn. [11] [Mr J. A. Parker]. [12] [Mr R. Burn: 6-in. O.S., 3317, by hill-shaded 1-in. map only a point on rising ridge, actual top being apparently ⅓m. S. by E., ⅛m. N. of a point 3367 on 6-in. map]. [13] [Note on Sir H. T. Munro's card index. Mr Colin Phillip says 4160 ap., as cairn is not on top "]. [14] Mr Hinxman. [15] It is difficult to decide what should be considered " tops " in the big plateau between Braeriach and Cairn Toul. [16] " Sgoran Dubh, S." of the 1st edn., now Sgùrr Gaoith, is locally known as Sgoran Dubh Bheag.

NAME.	HEIGHT. §	COUNTY. 1" O/S sheet No.	No. in order of Alt. Sep. Mt.	Top.	Map Ref.
SECTION 15.					
Meall Chuaich (*Meall na Cuaich*)	3120	Inverness 37	205	390	71 88
Càrn na Caim	3087	Inv., Perth ,,	223	424	67 82
A' Bhuidheanach Bheag (*Fuar Bheinn*)	3064	do. ,,	233	445	66 77
Meall a' Chaoruinn	3004	Inverness ,,	...	538	64 77
Glas Mheall Mòr	3037	Perth ... ,,	...	488	68 77
Càrn an Fhidleir or Càrn Ealar	3276	Ab.,Inv.,P'h ,,	134	244	90 84
An Sgarsoch	3300	Ab'n, Perth ,,	121	221	93 83
Druim Sgarsoch * ... ... (3100)	3128	do. ,,	...	381	94 83
Beinn Dearg	3304	Perth ... ,,	119	218	85 77
Beinn Gharbh ... ... (3000)	3050 ap.[1]	do. ,,	...	471	85 79
Càrn a' Chlamain *	3159	do. ... ,,	187	349	91 75
Beinn a' Ghlo (Ben-y-Gloe)—					
Càrn nan Gabhar (N.E. Top of B. a' Ghlo)	3671	do. ... 41 49	32	57	97 73
Àirgiod Bheinn * ... ... (3400)	3490 ap.[2]	do. ... ,, ,,	...	129	96 71
Braigh Coire Chruinn-bhalgain * (S.W. do.)	3505	do. ... 49	64	118	94 72
Càrn Liath	3193	do. ... ,,	177	320	93 69
Càrn an Righ	3377	do. ... 41	98	182	02 77
Glas Tulaichean (*Glas Thulachan*) ...	3445	do. ... ,,	74	144	05 76
Beinn Iutharn Mhòr (Ben Uarn Mòr) ...	3424	Ab'n, Perth ,,	85	160	04 79
do. Bheag (do. Beàg) ...	3121 [4]	Aberdeen ,,	...	387	06 79
Màm nan Càrn	3224 [4]	Perth ... ,,	...	289	05 78
Càrn Bhac, N.E. Top (*Top of Coire Bhourneasg*)	3098	Aberdeen ,,	217	417	05 83
do. S.W. Top	3014	Ab'n, Perth ,,	...	520	04 82
[Càrn a' Bhutha[12]]	3000 contour	Perth ... ,,	...	544	03 82
An Sòcach: (East end) Sòcach Mòr [5] ...	3073	Aberdeen ,,	230	440	09 80
do. (West end)	3059	do. ,,	...	452	08 80
Càrn a' Gheoidh (*Càrn a' Geoidhe*) ...	3194	Ab'n, Perth ,,	175	318	10 76
Càrn Bhinnein	3006	Perth ... ,,	...	532	09 76
Càrn nan Sac (. . . . *Sae*) ... ... (3000)	3000	Ab'n, Perth ,,	...	542	11 77
The Cairnwell	3059	do. ,,	238	453	13 77
Càrn Aosda	3003	Aberdeen ,,	276	539	13 79
SECTION 16.					
Glas Maol	3502	Forfar ... ,,	67	121	16 76
Meall Odhar	3019	Ab'n, Perth ,,	...	512	15 77
Little Glas Maol * [11]	3184	Forfar ,,	...	333	17 76
Creag Leacach	3238	Forf., Perth 41 49	152	279	15 74
Cairn of Claise (*Cairn na Glasha*) ...	3484	Ab'n, Forf. 41	68	130	18 79
Druim Mòr * [11]	3144	Forfar ,,	...	361	19 77
Càrn an Tuirc	3340	Aberdeen ,,	109	202	17 80
Tom Buidhe	3140	Forfar ,,	195	367	21 78
Tolmount (*Tolmont*)	3143	Ab'n, Forf. ,,	190	362	21 80
Crow Craigies *	3014	Forfar ,,	...	519	22 79
Cairn Bannoch	3314	Ab'n, Forf. ,,	115	213	22 82
Fafernie	3274	do. ,,	246	21 82	
Creag Leachdach [11] ... ... (3150)	3100 ap.[6]	Aberdeen ,,	...	414	21 81
Cairn of Gowal * [11] ... ... (3200)	3242	Ab'n, Forf. ,,	...	274	22 81
Craig of Gowal ... ... (3000)	3027	Forfar ,,	...	501	23 80
Broad Cairn	3268	Ab'n, Forf. ,,	141	254	24 81
Creag an Dubh-loch ... ... (3200)	3100 ap.[7]	Aberdeen ,,	...	415	23 82
Lochnagar Range—					
Lochnagar, Cac Càrn Beag	3786	do. ,,	20	33	24 86
do. Cairn (*Cac Carn Mòr, new 1-in. map*)	3768	do. ,,	...	37	24 85
Meall Coire na Saobhaidhe	3191	do. ,,	...	324	24 87
Cuidhe Cròm	3552	do. 41 42	...	102	26 85
Little Pap ... ... (3050)	3125 ap.[7]	do. ,, ,,	...	385	26 84
Meikle Pap	3211	do. ,, ,,	...	300	26 86
White Mounth—					
Càrn a' Choire Bhoidheach * [9] ... (3650)	3630 ap.[8]	do. 41	44	75	22 84
Creag a' Ghlas-uillt * ... ... (3500)	3495 ap.	do. ,,	...	128	24 84
[Stob an] Dubh Loch ‡ ... ... (3450)	3470 ap.[7]	do. ,,	...	135	23 83
Càrn an t-Sagairt Beag * ... ... (3400)	3424	do. ,,	...	161	21 84
Càrn an t-Sagairt Mòr [10]	3430	do. ,,	81	155	20 84
Mayar	3043	Forfar 41 49	249	478	24 73
Driesh	3105	do. 41 42 49	212	400	27 73
Mount Keen	3077	Ab'n, Forf. ,,42	229	436	41 87

* *Named only on the 6-inch map.*   † *Local name, not given on either O.S. map.*
‡ *New top, not in the original Tables.*   § *The 1-in. height is given in parenthesis if different from 6-in.*
[1] [Dr Corner].   [2] [Mr R. Burn].   [3] [On 6-in. sheet 110, Aberdeen, 170 yards N. by E. of acute angle in the county boundary marked 3096 on the 1-in. map].   [4] 150 yards S.S.W. of 3217 point on 1-in. map.   [5] On 1-in. map "An Socach" applies to both tops: on 6-in. "An Socach" is only the W. top, while the E. top is called "Socach Mòr." The name Socach Mòr on 1-in. map is ¾m. E. of top.   [6] [Estimate from the hill-shaded 1-inch map].   [7] Sir H. T. Munro.   [8] Sir H. T. Munro. On

Top No.	Position	Best Ascended From
	SECTION 15.	
390	1¼ m. E. of L. Cuaich	Dalwhinnie Ho., 5½ m. E.N.E.
424	2¾ m. E.S.E. from Dalwhinnie Hotel	do. 2¾ m.; Dalnaspidal Sta., 5¾ m.
445	⅞ m. E. from Meall a' Chaoruinn	Dalnaspidal Sta., 2¾ m.; Dalwhinnie Ho., 4½ m.
538	2¾ m. N. from Dalnaspidal Station	do. 2¾ m.; do. 4¼ m.
488	3¼ m. N.E. do.	do. 3¼ m.; do. 5½ m.
244	Bet. heads of Glen Feshie and Glen Tarf	Bynack Lod., 6 m.; Blair Ath., 11¾ m. N. by E.
221	1¾ m. E. by S. of Càrn an Fhidleir	do. 4¼ m.; do. 11¾ m. N.N.E.
381	¾ m. E. from An Sgarsoch	do. 3¾ m.; do. 12 m.
218	Head of Glen Bruar, E. side	Blair Atholl, 7¾ m. N. by W.; Struan, 8¼ m.
471	⅞ m. N. from Beinn Dearg	do. 9 m.; do. 9 m.
349	1½ m. N.W. from Forest Lodge, Glen Tilt	do. 6¾ m. N.N.E.
	Beinn a' Ghlo—	
57	8 m. N.E. of Blair Atholl	do. 8 m.; Pitlochry, 9½ m.
129	Shoulder, 1m. S.W. by S. from C. nan [Gabhar	do. 7 m.; do. 8½ m.
118	1⅝ m. W.S.W. from do.	do. 6½ m. N.E.; do. 9 m.
320	4¾ m. N.E. from Blair Atholl	do. 4½ m. N.E. by E.; Pitlochry, 7¼ m
182	1½ m. W.N.W. from Glas Tulaichean	Fealar Lod., 2¼ m.; Spital of Glens'e, 6¾ m. NW
144	5¼ m. N.W. from Spital of Glenshee	Spital of Glenshee, 5¼ m.
160	2 m. N. by W. from Glas Tulaichean	do. 7 m.; Inverey, 6½ m.; Braemar, 10 m.
387	1 m. E. by S. from Beinn Iutharn Mhòr	do. 6½ m.; do. 6½ m.; do. 9½ m.
288	⅞ m. S. by E. do.	do. 6½ m.
417	2½m. N. from do. (E. of Coire Bhearnaist)	Inverey, 4¼ m.; B'mar, 8 m.; Spital of G'shee 9m.
520	¾ m. W.S.W. from N.E. Top	do. 5 m.; do. 8¾ m.; do. 9 m.
544	⅝ m. S.W. from S.W. Top	do. 5½ m.; do. 8¾ m.; do. 8¾ m.
440	2½ m. E.N.E. from Beinn Iutharn Bheag	do. 5½ m.; do. 7½ m.; do. 6¾ m.
452	1½ m. E.N.E. do.	do. 5¾ m.; do. 8¼ m.; do. 6½ m.
318	3½ m. E. by N. from Glas Tulaichean	Spital of Glenshee, 4¼ m. N. by W.; B'mar, 9½m.
532	1 m. W.S.W. from Càrn a' Gheoidh	do. 4¼ m.; do. 10¼m.
542	¾ m. E. by N. do.	do. 4½ m.; do. 9¼ m.
453	½ m. W. by S. from summit of carriage road	Braemar-Blairgowrie. Spital of Glenshee 5 m.;
539	1 m. N. from Cairnwell	Sp. of Gl'shee, 6 m.; B'mar, 7½ m. [B'mar, 8¾ m.
	SECTION 16.	
121	Head of Glen Isla	Spital of Glenshee, 5½ m.; Tulchan (Glen Isla),
512	⅞ m. N.W. by W. from Glas Maol	do. 5½ m. [3 m.
333	¾ m. S.E. do.	do. 5½ m.
279	1½ m. S.S.W. do.	do. 4 m.
130	Hd. of G. Isla, 2m. N.E. by N.of Glas Maol	Spital of Glenshee, 7½ m.; Braemar, 8 m.; L.
361	1 m. S.S.E. from Cairn of Claise	Callater Lo., 3½ m.; Kirkton of Glenisla, 10½m.
202	2 m. S.S.W. from head of Loch Callater	Loch Callater Lodge, 2½ m.; Braemar, 7 m.
367	Head of Glen Doll	Clova, 8 m. NW; L. Call. Lo, 4¼m; B'mar, 8¾m.
362	Hd. Gl. Callater, ¾ m. NNW of Tom B'dhe	do. 8½ m.; do. 3½ m.; do. 8m.
519	¾ m. E. from Tolmount	do. 7¾ m.; do. 4 m.; do. 8½m.
213	Head of Glen Muick, ½ m. ENE of Fafernie	do. 8¾ m.; do. 3 m.; do. 7m.
246	Hd. Gl. Callater, 2 m. ESE of L. Callater	do. 9 m.; do. 2¾ m.; do. 7 m.
414	do. ½ m. SW by S of Fafernie	do. 9 m.; do. 2¾ m.; do. 7m.
274	⅝ m. S.E. by S. from Cairn Bannoch	do. 8¼ m.; do. 3½ m.; do. 7¾m.
501	1¼ m. S.S.E. do.	do. 7½ m.; do. 4 m.; do. 8¼m.
254	2½ m. S. from Lochnagar (Cairn)	Clova, 7½ m.; L. Callater Lo., 4¼ m.; Spital of
415	S. cliffs of Dubh L.; ⅝ m. N.W. of Br. C'n	Glen Muick, 4¾ m.
	Lochnagar Range—	
33	5¾ m. S. from Balmoral	Balmoral, 5¾m.; Braemar, 6½m.; Ballater, 10m.;
37	⅓ m. S.S.E. from Cac Càrn Beag	Spital of Glenmuick, 4m.; L. Callater Lo. 4¼m.
324	1 m. N. by W. from Lochnagar (Cairn)	Balmoral, 5 m.; Braemar, 6¼ m.; Ballater, 9½ m.
102	1 m. E.S.E. do.	do. 6¾ m.; do. 7¼ m.; do. 9¾ m.
385	½ m. S.E. from Cuidhe Cròm	do. 6¾ m.; do. 8¼ m.; do. 9¾ m.
300	1 m. E.N.E. from Lochnagar (Cairn)	do. 5¾ m.; do. 7½ m.; do. 9¼ m.
	White Mounth—	
75	1⅜ m. S.W. by W. of Lochnagar (Cairn)	Braemar, 6¼ m.; Spital of Glenmuick, 5 m.;
128	1 m. S. by W. do.	Ballater, 11m.; L. Call. Lo., 3m. [Muick, 4½.
135	1¼ m. N. from Dubh Loch	Braemar, 7¼m.; L. Call. Lo., 3¾m.; Spital Gl.
161	⅝ m. E.N.E. of Càrn an t-Sagairt Mòr	do. 5¾m.; do. 2½m.; do. 5½m.
155	2 m. E. from foot of Loch Callater	do. 5½m. S.E. do. 1¾m.; do. 6¼m
478	Hd. Glen Prosen, 5½ m. W. of Clova	Clova, 5½m; Inchmill (Gl. Prosen), 4¾m; Gl. Doll
400	3½ m. W. of Clova	do. 3½ m. do. 3¾ m. [Lodge, 3 m.
436	6 m. S.S.E. from Ballater	Ballater, 6 m.

the 6-in. O.S. there is a point 3571, close to the crags over L. nan Eun, just N. of the Lochnagar track from Braemar: the hill rises considerably to S. of the track. 9 Called Cairn of Corbreach on Baddeley's and Bartholomew's maps. 10 Called Cairn Taggart on Baddeley's and Bartholomew's maps. 11 In the Eastern Grampians it is specially difficult to decide what are separate mountains, tops, or merely shoulders. Little Glas Maol, Druim Mòr, Creag Leachdach, and Cairn of Gowal are all very doubtful tops. H.T.M. 12 [New 1-in. map has a new top Càrn a' Bhutha (3000 cont.: 6-in. map only, " trig. station " mark). [See "Additional Notes", p. 43].

SECTION 17.

NAME.	HEIGHT.	POSITION 1" O/S sheet No.		Ascended from Slig.[6]	Gl. Br.[7]	Sep. Mt.	Top.	Map Ref.
The Cuillin—		*Isle of Skye, Inverness-shire.*						
Blaven (*Blath Bheinn*) ...	3042	5¾ m. S.S.E. of Slig'n Inn	25 33	5¼ m.	...	250	479	53 21
Sgùrr nan Gillean ...	3167	3 m. S. by W. do.	,,	3 m.	...	184	342	47 25
Am Bàsteir[2] (*Bhasteir*)	[1]3050ap	½ m. W. of Sgùrr nan Gillean	,,	3¼ m.	...	246	469	46 25
Bhasteir Tooth † ‡ ...	[1]3000ap	Immediately W. of Am Bàsteir	,,	3¼ m.	...	...	543	46 25
Bruach na Frithe ...	3143	⅜ m. W. of Sgùrr nan Gillean	,,	3⅓ m.	...	191	363	46 25
Sgùrr a' Fionn Choire† ‡	3050ap	150 yds. S.W. of Am Bàsteir	,,	3¼ m.	...	...	472	46 25
Sgùrr a' Mhadaidh ‡S.W.p'k	3014 [3]	1⅓ m. SW of Bruach na Frithe	,,	4¼ m.	2¾ m.	270	521	45 23
Sgùrr a'Ghreadaidh, N. Top	3197	⅓ m. SSW of Sg. a'Mhadaidh,	,,	5 m.	2½ m.	173	314	44 23
do. S. Top ‡	[1] 3180ap	do. [SW peak	,,	5 m.	2½ m.	...	335	44 22
Sgùrr na Banachdich,[4] N. Top	3167	150 yds S by W of Sg. Thorm'd,	,,	5½ m.	2 m.	185	343	43 22
do. Centre Top ‡	3104	100 yds. S. by E. of North Top	,,	5½ m.	2 m.	...	404	44 22
Sgùrr Thormaid * ‡	3007	½ m. S.W. of Sg. Ghreadaidh	,,	5¼ m.	2 m.	...	529	44 22
Sgùrr Dearg—								
Inaccessible Pinnacle	3254	⅝ m. SSE of Sg. na Banachdich	,,	5¾ m.	2 m.	147	265	44 21
Cairn (O.S. point) ...	3234	NW of Inaccessible, close to it	,,	5¾ m.	2 m.	...	281	44 21
Sgùrr Mhic Coinnich ...	3107	½ m. SE by E of Sgùrr Dearg	,,	6 m.	2½ m.	210	397	45 21
Sgùrr Alasdair	3309	⅔ m. S.E. of Sgùrr Dearg	,,	6 m.	2½ m.	117	216	45 20
Sgùrr Thearlaich[5] ...	[1] 3230ap	100 yds. NE of Sgùrr Alasdair	,,	6 m.	2½ m.	...	285	45 20
Sgùrr Squmain (*Sgumain*)	3104	200 yds. S.W. do.	,,	6¼ m.	2⅓ m.	...	401	44 20
Sgùrr Dubh Mòr[8] ...	3089	½ m. E. by S. do.	,,	6 m.	3 m.	221	422	45 20
Sgùrr Dubh na Da Bheinn*[9]	3069	¼ m. W. by S. of Sg. Dubh Mòr,	,,	6¼ m.	2¾ m.	...	441	45 20
Sgùrr nan Eag	3037	⅝ m. S by E of Sg. Dubh na [Da Bheinn	33 34	6¾ m.	3¼ m.	255	489	45 19
Island of Mull, Argyllshire—								
Ben More	3169	7 m. S.S.W. of Salen, Mull	45	Salen, Mull, 7m.		182	340	52 33

* *Named only on 6-inch map.* ‡ *Local name, not on either O.S. map.* ‡ *New top, not in 1st edn.*

[1] The approximate heights are from careful aneroid measurements by Dr Norman Collie and others. The contours for the Cuillin Hills (so spelt on the O.S. maps) on the 1-in. map cannot be relied on, and are therefore omitted here. For instance, the height 3197 for Sgùrr a' Ghreadaidh is given in a 2750 contour. [2] Also known as Sgùrr Dubh a' Bhàsteir. [3] Sgùrr a' Mhadaidh consists of 4 peaks, 2970, 2880, 2910, and 3014. The highest or S.W. peak has two tops, both about the same height. [4] Also spelt Banachaig. [5] Formerly called the N.E. Peak of Sgùrr Alasdair. [6] Sligachan Inn. [7] Glen Brittle House. [8] Sgùrr Dubh, Central Peak, 1st edn. [9] Sgùrr Dubh, W. Peak, 1st edn.

Tops Promoted to be Separate Mountains, in the Revised Tables:—

A' Gruagach (now Na Gruagaichean)	3442 ft.	Section 5
Bhasteir (now Am Basteir)	3050 ap.	,, 17
Fuar Bheinn (now A' Bhuidheanach Bheag)	3064	,, 15
Meall an Teanga	3050 ap.	,, 7
Sgùrr Mhic Coinnich (*New Top and separate Mountain*)	3107	,, 17
An Garbhanach (in place of An Gearanach) (*restored to original*, 1933)...	3200 ap.	,, 5
Càrn Bhac, N.E. Top (Top of Coire Bhourneasg) in place of S.W. Top[10]	3098	,, 15
(Creag a' Choir' Aird), South. Ridge (New Top, in place of 3188 Top)[10]	3210 ap.	,, 8
Creag an Lochan (now [Stob] Poite Coire Ardair) in place of Crom Leathad[10]	3460	,, 6
Creag Toll a' Choin (in place of Maoile Lunndaidh)[10]	3295 ap.	,, 9
Meall Glas (in place of B. Dheiceach, being highest point)	3139	,, 3
Sgiath Chùil (in place of Meall Chuirn, being highest point)	3050 ap.	,, 3

Separate Mountains Reduced to Tops, in the Revised Tables:—

Beinn a' Chuirn	3020	Section 3
,, Iutharn Bheag	3096	,, 15
Bidean an Eoin Deirg	3430	,, 9
Càrn Bhinnein	3006	,, 15
,, Eas	3556	,, 14
Creag Dubh	3102	,, 9
,, na Dala Moire	3189	,, 14
,, na Leacainn, S. Top (now Creag na Leth-choin)	3448	,, 14
Glas Mheal Mòr	3037	,, 15
Meall a' Chaoruinn	3004	,, 15
Sgòrr Chòinnich	3040	,, 5
Sgòr an Lochan Uaine (Cairn Toul)	4095 ap.	,, 14
Sgùrr na Lapaich (Mam Sodhail)	3401	,, 8

Tops Deleted from the Tables, as not having sufficient claims to be "tops":—

An Socach (Ben Wyvis)	3295	Section 12
Beinn a' Chaoruinn, Middle Top (Glen Spean)	3394	,, 6
,, na Socaich (Stob Coire an Easain)	3000 cont.	,, 5
Big Brae (Ben Avon)	3100	,, 14
Blath Bheinn, S. Top (Blaven)	3031	,, 17
Càrn Ballach, S.W. Top (Monadh Liadth Mts.)	3009	,, 6
Creag a' Bhragit (Stobinian)	3000 cont.	,, 1
,, Meaghaidh, E. Top	3594	,, 6
Cruach Ardran, N.E. Top	3477	,, 1
Druim nan Bo (Meall Tionail)	3005	,, 14
Leachd Riach (Monadh Mor)	3250 cont.	,, 14
Sròn dha Murchdi (Ben Lawers)	3040 ap.	,, 3
,, a' Ghaothair (Creag Meaghaidh)	3150 ap.	,, 6
Top between Cruach Ardran and Stob Garbh	3034	,, 1
Top of Coire Dubh (Beinn Creachan)	3145	,, 3

[10] Being highest point.

Table II.   Arranged in Order of Altitude.   43

TABLE II.

THE 3000-FEET TOPS ARRANGED IN ORDER OF ALTITUDE.

* Named only on 6-inch map.   † Local name, not in O.S. maps.   ‡ New top, not in 1st edn.
The figures in brackets are heights in the original Tables which differ.
In the Revised Tables, "[Stob]" represents " Top of," " Top above," etc., in the 1st edition.

No. in order of Alt. Sep. Mt.	Top.	Height.	Name.	Height, 1st edn.	Sect. in Table I.
1	1	4406	Ben Nevis		5
2	2	4300	Ben Macdui (Macdhui)		14
3	3	4248	Braeriach		14
...	4	4244	Ben Macdui (Macdhui) (N. Top)		14
4	5	4241	Cairn Toul		14
...	6	4149	Braeriach (S. plateau)		14
...	7	4095	[Stob] Coire Sputan Dearg (Ben Macdhui)		14
...	8	4095(ap.)	Sgòr an Lochan Uaine * (Cairn Toul)		14
5	9	4084	Cairngorm		14
6	10	4060	Aonach Beag (Lochaber)		5
...	11	4036	[Stob] Coire an Lochain (Braeriach)		14
7	12	4012	Càrn Mòr Dearg		5
8	13	3999	Aonach Mòr		5
...	14	3989	[Stob] Coire an t-Saighdeir * (Cairn Toul)		14
9	15	3984	Ben Lawers		3
...	16	3983	Cairn Lochan (Cairngorm)		14
...	17	3961	Càrn Dearg (N.W., Ben Nevis)		5
10	18	3924	Beinn a' Bhuird (N. top)		14
11	19	3883	Beinn Mheadhoin (N.E. top)		14
12	20	3877	Càrn Eige (L. Affric)		8
...	21	3875	Sròn na Lairig (Braeriach)		14
...	22	3873	Càrn Dearg Meadhonach	[3875]	5
13	23	3862	Mam Sodhail (Mam Soul)		8
...	24	3860	Beinn a' Bhuird (S. top)		14
14	25	3858	Stob Choire Claurigh (S. top)		5
...	26	3856	[Stob] Coire an t-Sneachda *		14
15	27	3843	Ben Avon, Leabaidh an Daimh Bhuidhe		14
16	28	3843	Ben More (Perthshire)		1
17	29	3827	Am Binnein (Perthshire)		1
...	30	3811	Cnap a' Chleirich (B. a' Bhuird)		14
18	31	3795	Beinn Bhrotain		14
19	32	3788	Derry Cairngorm		14
20	33	3786	Lochnagar—Cac Càrn Beag		16
21	34	3773	Sgùrr na Làpaich (L. Mullardoch)		9
...	35	3772	Cnap Coire na Spreidhe		14
22	36	3771	Sgùrr nan Ceathreamhnan (Centre top)		8
...	37	3768	Lochnagar (Cairn)		16
23	38	3766	Bidean nam Bian		4
24	39	3757	Ben Alder		5
...	40	3753	Creag na h-Eige		8
..	41	3750	Beinn Mheadhoin (S.W. top)		14
...	42	3737	Fiacaill a' Choire Chais		14
...	43	3736	Sgùrr nan Ceathreamhnan (W. top)	[3737]	8
...	44	3729	Ben Avon (S.W. top)		14
...	45	3725	[Stob] Coire Dhomhnuill ‡		8
...	46	3720(ap.)	Stob Coire na Ceannain		5
...	47	3719(ap.)	Stob Choire Claurigh (N. top) ‡		5
25	48	3708	Beinn Laoigh		1
...	49	3705	Sròn Garbh (Càrn Eige)	[3500 cont.]	8
26	50	3700	Creag Meaghaidh		6
27	51	3700	Binnein Mòr (Glen Nevis)		5
28	52	3696	An Riabhachan (N.E. top)		9
29	53	3689	Ben Cruachan		4
30	54	3688	Geal Chàrn * (N.W. of Ben Alder)		5
31	55	3673	A' Chràlaig	[3676]	8
...	56	3673	Cairn Etchachan *		14
32	57	3671	Beinn a' Ghlo—Càrn nan Gabhar		15
...	58	3662	Mullach Lochan nan Gabhar		14
33	59	3661	Meall Garbh (Ben Lawers)		3
34	60	3659	Stob Choire an Laoigh *		5
35	61	3658	Stob Coire Easain (L. Treig)		5
36	62	3658	Sgòr Gaoith		14
37	63	3657(ap.)	Beinn Ghlas (Ben Lawers)		3
...	64	3657	Stob Coire nan Lochan (Glencoe)		4
38	65	3651	Monadh Mòr		14
39	66	3646	Aonach Beag (Alder district) (3647, 1-inch map)		5
40	67	3646	Tom a' Chòinich		8
...	68	3644	[Stob] Coire Bhealaich *		5
...	69	3643	An Stùc *		3

Sep.	Mt.	Top	HEIGHT.	NAME.	Height, 1st edn.	Sect. in Table I.
...		70	3640(ap.)	Fiacaill Coire an t-Sneachda *	[3500 cont.]	14
41	71		3637	Sgùrr Mòr (Fannaich)		11
42	72		3636	Clach Leathad—Meall a' Bhùiridh		4
43	73		3635	Sgùrr nan Conbhairean		8
...		74	3635	Sgòran Dubh Mòr	[3636]	14
44	75		3630(ap.)	Càrn a' Choire Bhoidheach *		16
...		76	3629	Creagan a' Choire Etchachan	[3500 cont.]	14
...		77	3627	Stob a' Choire Lèith *	[3629]	5
...		78	3625	Stùc Gharbh Mhòr		14
...		79	3621	Stob an t-Sluichd		14
...		80	3621	Stob Coire nam Beith † (Bidean)		4
45	81		3614	Mullach Fraoch-choire		8
...		82	3611	Stob Dearg † (Ben Cruachan)		4
46	83		3611	Beinn Eibhinn (Alder district)		5
47	84		3610	Stob a' Choire Mheadhoin		5
...		85	3609	Caisteal * (Lochaber)		5
...		86	3606	Ciste Dhubh * (Mam Sodhail)		8
48	87		3603	Sgùrr Chòinnich Mòr		5
49	88		3602	Clach Leathad		4
50	89		3601	Sgùrr a' Mhaim		5
...		90	3600	Crèise † (Clach Leathad)		4
...		91	3591	Puist Coire Ardair * (*Crags above* ....)		6
...		92	3591(ap.)	Sgùrr nan Clachan Geala *	[3250 cont.]	9
51	93		3581	Sgùrr nan Clach Geala		11
...		94	3580(ap.)	[Stob] an Cùl Choire *		5
52	95		3574	Bynack More		14
53	96		3569	Beinn a' Chlachair (Alder district)		5
54	97		3565	Stob Ghabhar		4
...		98	3563	Stob Dubh an Eàs Bhig (Ben Avon)	[3250 cont.]	14
...		99	3556	Càrn Eàs		14
55	100		3554	Sgùrr a' Choire Ghlais		9
56	101		3553	Beinn a' Chaorruinn (Cairngorms)		14
...		102	3552	Cuidhe Cròm * (Lochnagar)		16
...		103	3551	[Stob] Coire Etchachan		14
...		104	3550(ap.)	Fiacaill na Leth-choin † ‡		14
57	105		3547	Schichallion		3
58	106		3547	Beinn Dearg (Ross-shire)		12
...		107	3545	Stob Coire an Easain (Glen Nevis)		5
59	108		3541	Ben Starav		4
60	109		3540	Beinn a' Chreachain		3
...		110	3534	Sròn Riach * (Ben Macdhui)		14
...		111	3533	Stob Bac an Fhurain		14
61	112		3530(ap.)	Meall Corranaich		3
62	113		3530	Beinn Heasgarnich		3
...		114	3529	Stob Coire Cath na Sine *		5
63	115		3524	Beinn Dòrain	[3523]	3
...		116	3508	[Stob] Coire Coulavie *		8
...		117	3506	Mam Coire Easain * (Clach Leathad)		4
64	118		3505	Braigh Coire Chruinn-bhalgain * (B. a' Ghlo)		15
65	119		3505	Beinn Mhòr—Sgùrr Fhuaran		8
66	120		3503	An Socach * (L. Lungard)		9
67	121		3502	Glas Maol		16
...		122	3500(cont.)	A' Chioch ‡ (Beinn a' Bhuird)		14
...		123	3500 ,,	An Tudair		8
...		124	3497	Beinn Fhada (Glencoe) Stob Co. Sgreamhach† (Bidean)		4
...		125	3497	Stob Coire an Lochan (Am Binnein)		1
...		126	3496	Creag Mhòr (Creag Meaghaidh)		6
...		127	3496(ap.)	Stùc Mòr †	[3250 cont.]	8
...		128	3495(ap.)	Creag a' Ghlas-uillt * (Lochnagar)	[3450 ap.]	16
...		129	3490(ap.)	Airgiod Bheinn * (Beinn a' Ghlo)	[3250 cont.]	15
68	130		3484	Cairn of Claise		16
...		131	3484(ap.)	Rudha na Spreidhe *	[3250 cont.]	9
69	132		3483	An Teallach—Bidein a' Ghlas Thuill		11
...		133	3475	Binnein Mòr (S. top) (Top of Coire nan Laoigh) *		5
...		134	3474	Sgùrr Fiona (An Teallach)		11
...		135	3470(ap.)	[Stob an] Dubh Loch ‡		16
...		136	3462	Creag a' Chaoruinn (Mam Sodhail Dist.)		8
70	137		3460	[Stob] Poite Coire Ardair (W. top) (*Creag an Lochain*)		6
71	138		3456	Liathach—Spidean a' Choire Lèith		10
72	139		3452	Sgùrr a' Chaorachain		9
73	140		3452	Toll Creagach †		8
...		141	3450(ap.)	Tom a' Chòinich Beag †		8
...		142	3450(ap.)	Little Cairngorm † ‡		14
...		143	3448	Creag an Leth-choin (S. top)	[3450]	14
74	144		3445	Glas Tulaichean		15
75	145		3443	Càrn Bàn Mòr (L. Einich)		14
...		146	3443	An Leth-Chreag *		8
76	147		3443	Mullach Coire an Iubhair (Geal Chàrn)		5
77	148		3442	Na Gruagaichean		5

Table II. Arranged in Order of Altitude. 45

No. in order of Alt. Sep.Mt.	Top.	HEIGHT.	NAME.	Height, 1st edn.	Sect in Table I.
...	149	3441	[Stob] Poite Coire Ardair (E. top) (*Crom Leathad*) *		6
78	150	3439	Sgùrr Fhuar-thuill ...		9
79	151	3437	Beinn a' Chaoruinn (S. top) (Glen Spean) ...		6
...	152	3435	Mullach Fraoch-choire (N.E. top)		8
80	153	3433	Chno Dearg ...		5
...	154	3430	Bidean an Eòin Deirg ...	:.	9
81	155	3430	Càrn an t-Sagairt Mòr ...		16
...	156	3430	Creag an Fhithich *		3
82	157	3429	Ben Wyvis—Glas Leathad Mòr		12
83	158	3428	Cruach Ardrain	[3477]	1
84	159	3425	Stob Coir' an Albannaich		4
85	160	3424	Beinn Iutharn Mhòr		15
...	161	3424	Càrn an t-Sagairt Beag *		16
...	162	3422	Beinn a' Chaoruinn (N. top) (Glen Spean) ...		6
86	163	3421	Meall nan Tarmachan		3
87	164	3419	Càrn Mairg (Glen Lyon)		3
88	165	3410	Sgùrr na Ciche		7
89	166	3407	Meall Ghaordie		3
...	167	3406	An Riabhachan (W. top)		9
90	168	3404	Beinn Achaladair (N. top)		3
...	169	3404	Na Gruagaichean (N.W. top)		5
...	170	3401	Sgùrr na Làpaich (Mam Sodhail)		8
91	171	3400(ap.)	Càrn a' Mhaim ...	[3329]	14
92	172	3395	Gleouraich		7
93	173	3391	Càrn Dearg (Alder Dist.)		5
...	174	3388(ap.)	Sròn a' Cha-no *	[3250 cont.]	14
94	175	3387	Creag Mhòr (Loch Lyon)		3
95	176	3383	Beinn Fhada (Ben Attow)		8
96	177	3382	Am Bodach (Glen Nevis)		5
...	178	3381	Stob an Fhir-Bhogha * (B. Heasgarnich)		3
...	179	3380(ap.)	Lord Berkeley's Seat (An Teallach)	[3300 ap.]	11
97	180	3378	Sgùrr a' Bhealaich Dheirg		8
...	181	3378	Creag Ghorm a' Bhealaich		9
98	182	3377	Càrn an Righ		15
99	183	3374	Beinn Oss ...		1
...	184	3372	Stob Coire Dheirg * (B. Starav)		4
100	185	3370	Càrn Gorm (Càrn Mairg)		3
101	186	3370	Sgùrr na Ciste Duibhe (B. Mhòr)		8
...	187	3369(ap.)	Meall Garbh * (Meall nan Tarmachan)		3
...	188	3365	Creag an Leth-choin (N. top)		14
102	189	3365	Sgùrr a' Mhaoraich		7
...	190	3365(ap.)	Garbh Chiòch Mhòr		7
103	191	3362	B. a' Bheithir—Sgòrr Dhearg ...		4
...	192	3360(ap.)	Corrag Bhuidhe * (An Teallach)		11
...	193	3358	Mullach an Rathain		10
...	194	3354	West Meur Gorm Craig *		14
104	195	3354	Beinn Chaluim (N. top)		3
...	196	3350(ap.)	Sgùrr Creag an Eich * (An Teallach)		11
...	197	3348	Càrn Dearg (S.W.) (Ben Nevis)		5
105	198	3345	A' Chòinneach *		14
106	199	3345	Buachaille Etive Mòr—Stob Dearg		4
107	200	3343	Ladhar Bheinn ...		7
108	201	3342	Aonach air Chrith		7
109	202	3340	Càrn an Tuirc		16
110	203	3338	Mullach Clach a' Bhlair		14
111	204	3333	Beinn Bheòil		5
...	205	3330	Stacan Dubha * ‡	[3329]	14
112	206	3327	Mullach Coire Mhic Fhearchair		11
...	207	3326	Sgùrr na Fearstaig		9
...	208	3326	Beinn a' Chaorruinn Bheag * (Cairngorms)		14
...	209	3320(ap.)	Sròn Garbh (B. Alder Forest)	[3206]	5
113	210	3318	Beinn Ime		1
114	211	3317	The Saddle		7
...	212	3315(ap.)	Meall a' Bhàrr (Càrn Mairg) ...	[3250 cont.]	3
115	213	3314	Cairn Bannoch ...		16
...	214	3312	Drochaid Glas *		4
116	215	3309	Beinn Eighe—Ruadh-stac Mòr		10
117	216	3309	Sgùrr Alasdair	[3210 ap.]	17
118	217	3306	Beinn Udlamain		5
119	218	3304	Beinn Dearg (Atholl)		15
120	219	3303	The Devil's Point		14
...	220	3303	Bràigh a' Choire Bhig ...		9
121	221	3300	An Sgarsoch		15
...	222	3300(ap.)	Sgòr Iuthàrn	[3250 cont.]	5
...	223	3300(ap.)	Drochaid an Tuill Easaich *	[3250 cont.]	8
...	224	3300(ap.)	Sgòr an Iubhair	[3250 cont.]	5
...	225	3299	Meall Coire Choille-rais		6
122	226	3298	Càrn Liath (Creag Meaghaidh)		6
...	227	3295	Mullach Fraoch-choire (S. top)		8

No. in order of Alt. Sep.Mt.	Top.	HEIGHT.	NAME.	Height, 1st edn.	Sect. in Table I.
123	228	3295	Creag Toll a' Choin		9
...	229	3294	Maoile Lunndaidh (Loch Monar)		9
124	230	3294	Beinn Fhionnlaidh (Ross-shire)		8
...	231	3291	Gleouraich (E. top)		7
125	232	3290	Sgùrr Mòr (L. Quoich)		7
...	233	3288	Beinn Achaladair (S. top) ... ... ᵀ..		3
126	234	3285	Tigh Mòr na Seilge (S.S.W. top)		8
127	235	3284	Sgòrr Dhonuill (B. a' Bheithir)		4
128	236	3284	Aonach Meadhoin †		8
129	237	3283	Beinn an Dòthaidh		3
...	238	3282	Creag nan Clachan Geala *		8
130	239	3282	Sgùrr an Lochain (Glen Shiel)		7
131	240	3280	Meall Greigh		3
132	241	3279	Sgùrr Eilde Mòr		5
...	242	3276	Tigh Mòr na Seilge (Centre top)		8
133	243	3276	A' Chailleach (Fannaich)		11
134	244	3276	Càrn an Fhidleir or Càrn Ealar		15
135	245	3274	Stob Bàn (Glen Nevis)		5
...	246	3274	Fafernie		16
136	247	3273	Ben More, Assynt		13
137	248	3272	Stob Diamh † (Cruachan)		4
...	249	3272	Aonach Eagach * (Stob Ghabhar)		4
138	250	3272	Sgùrr an Doire Leathain		7
...	251	3270	Sgùrr na Càrnach (Sgùrr Fhuaran)		8
139	252	3268	Spidean Mialach		7
140	253	3268	Meall Dubhag		14
141	254	3268	Broad Cairn		16
...	255	3265(ap.)	Beinn nan Eachan (W. top) (Tarmachans) ...		3
142	256	3265	An Caisteal (Glen Falloch)		1
...	257	3264	Càrn Beag Dearg (3265, 1-*in.* map)		5
...	258	3262	Mullach Cadha Rainich † (Mam Sodhail) ...		8
...	259	3261	Meall Liath * (Càrn Mairg range)		3
143	260	3260	Sgùrr Choinnich (L. Monar)		9
...	261	3260	Creag a' Chaoruinn † (L. Cluanie)		8
144	262	3258	Sgòr na h-Ulaidh		4
145	263	3258	Glas Bheinn Mhòr (L. Etive)		4
146	264	3254	Sgùrr na Ruaidhe (Glen Strath Farrar) ...		9
147	265	3254	Sgùrr Dearg (" Inaccessible Pinnacle ")	[3250 ap.]	17
...	266	3253	Càrn nam Fiaclan		9
148	267	3251	Càrn nan Gobhar (S. of Glen Strath Farrar)		9
...	268	3250	An Cearcallach (Creag Meaghaidh)		6
...	269	3250(ap.)	Stob na Doire * (Buachaille Etive Mòr) ...		4
...	270	3250 (cont.)	Stùc Bheag †		8
...	271	3250 ,,	Stob Coire an Fhir Dhuibh *		5
...	272	3250 ,,	Sròn Garbh Choire (Creag Meagdaidh) ...	[3248]	6
149	273	3242	Beinn Eunaich		4
...	274	3242	Cairn of Gowal *		16
150	275	3242	Càrn nan Gobhar (N. of Glen Strath Farrar)		9
...	276	3241	Sgùrr an Fhuarail		8
...	277	3240	Sròn a' Ghearrain (Stob Ghabhar)		4
151	278	3240(ap.)	Sgùrr Breac		11
152	279	3238	Creag Leacach		16
...	280	3236	Beinn Chaluim (S. top)		3
...	281	3234	Sgùrr Dearg (Ordnance point)		17
153	282	3234	Cona-mheall (Assynt)		13
154	283	3234	Lurg Mhòr		9
155	284	3232	B. Alligin—Sgùrr Mhòr		10
...	285	3230(ap.)	Sgùrr Thearlaich * ‡		17
156	286	3224	Gaor Bheinn or Gulvain (N. top)		7
157	287	3224	Ben Vorlich (Loch Earn)		2
...	288	3224	Màm nan Càrn		15
158	289	3222	Druim Shionnach		7
...	290	3220(ap.)	Spidean Coire nan Clach †		10
...	291	3220(ap.)	Sgùrr an Lochan Uaine ‡ (Derry Cairngorm)		14
159	292	3219	Stob Coire a' Chairn *		5
160	293	3218	Ciste Dhubh		8
161	294	3217	Slioch	[3260 ap.]	11
162	295	3217	Stob Bàn (Loch Treig Dist.)		5
...	296	3217	Sàil Mhòr (B. Eighe)		10
...	297	3215	Stob Garbh † (Cruachan)		4
163	298	3215	Beinn a' Chochuill		4
164	299	3214	Maol Chinn-dearg		7
...	300	3211	Meikle Pap		16
165	301	3211	Stob Coire Sgriodain (N. top)	[3210]	5
166	302	3210(ap.)	Sgairneach Mhòr	[3160]	5
167	303	3210(ap.)	(Creag a' Choir' Aird), Southern top *	[3000 cont.]	8
...	304	3207	Stob a' Ghlais Choire * (Clach Leathad)		4
168	305	3204	Beinn Dubhchraig		1
169	306	3200(ap.)	Creag Mhòr (Càrn Mairg)		3

Table II. Arranged in order of Altitude.   47

No. in order of Alt. Sep.Mt.	Top.	Height.	Name.	Height, 1st edn.	Sect. in Table I.
170	307	3200(ap.)	Cona' Mheall (L. Broom)		12
171	308	3200 ,,	Meall Garbh (Càrn Mairg)		3
...	309	3200 ,,	Ben More, Assynt (S. top)		13
172	310	3200 ,,	An Gearanach *		5
...	311	3200 ,,	An Garbhanach		5
...	312	3200 ,,	Bidean Toll a' Mhuic † (Liathach)		10
...	313	3197	Meall Garbh (Loch Treig)		5
173	314	3197	Sgùrr a' Ghreadaidh (N. top)		17
174	315	3196	Ben Sgritheall (Sgriol)		7
...	316	3196	The Saddle (W. top)		7
...	317	3195(ap.)	Creag a' Chaoruinn * (Sgùrr na Làpaich) [3000 cont.]		9
175	318	3194	Càrn a' Gheoidh		15
176	319	3194	Sgùrr Bàn (N.E. of L. Maree)		11
177	320	3193	Càrn Liath (B. a' Ghlo)		15
...	321	3193	Meall Buidhe (Rannoch)		3
178	322	3192	Ben Lomond		1
179	323	3192(ap.)	Meall nan Ceapràichean		12
...	324	3191	Meall Coire na Saobhaidhe		16
...	325	3190	Meall Mòr		9
180	326	3189	Stùc a' Ch		2
...	327	3189	Creag an Dail Mhor *		14
...	328	3188	Creag a' Choir' Aird * (N. top)		8
...	329	3188	Sgùrr Bàn (Eighe)		10
181	330	3185	A' Mharconaich		5
...	331	3185	Meall Buidhe † (Cairngorms)		14
...	332	3184	Diollaid Coire Eindart *		14
...	333	3184	Little Glas Maol *		16
...	334	3180	Meall an-t-Snaim *		6
...	335	3180(ap.)	Sgùrr a' Ghreadaidh (S. top) ‡		17
...	336	3177	A' Bhuidheanach		6
...	337	3176	Glas Mheall Mòr (An Teallach)		11
...	338	3175	Sgùrr Chòinnich Beag		5
...	339	3174	Sròn nan Giubhas (Stob Ghabhar)		4
182	340	3169	Ben More (Mull)		17
183	341	3168	Sgòr nam Fiannaidh		5
184	342	3167	Sgùrr nan Gillean		17
185	343	3167	Sgùrr na Banachdich (N. top)		17
...	344	3165	Sgùrr a' Bhuic *		5
186	345	3164	Sgùrr Thuilm		7
...	346	3163	Sròn an Isean † (Cruachan)		4
...	347	3160	Sgùrr an Fhir Duibhe † (B. Eighe)		10
...	348	3160(ap.)	Stob an Fhuarain *		4
187	349	3159	Càrn a' Chlamain *		15
188	350	3154	Ben Klibreck	[3164]	13
...	351	3150(ap.)	Stob Coire Gaibhre *		5
...	352	3150 ,,	Meall Dearg † (Liathach)		10
...	353	3150 ,,	Sgùrr nan Ceathreamhnan (E. top) ‡ ...		8
...	354	3150 ,,	Ceum na h-Aon Choise *		8
...	355	3149	Toll Creagach (W. top) (Top N. of Allt Toll Easa)		8
...	356	3148	Gaor Bheinn or Gulvain (S. top)		7
...	357	3148	Stob Garbh (Cruach Ardrain)		1
...	358	3148	Càrn na Criche		11
...	359	3146	Stob nan Clach *		3
189	360	3144	Stuchd an Lochain		3
...	361	3144	Druim Mòr *		16
190	362	3143	Tolmount		16
191	363	3143	Bruach na Frithe		17
192	364	3142	Sgòrr Ruadh (Strathcarron)	[3141]	10
193	365	3141	Beinn nan Aighean		4
194	366	3140	Càrn Ghluasaid		8
195	367	3140	Tom Buidhe		16
...	368	3140	Sgùrr Eilde Beag *		5
...	369	3140	Meall na Dige		1
196	370	3139	Meall Glas (Glen Dochart)		3
197	371	3139	Beinn Fhionnlaidh (Glen Creran)		4
...	372	3138	Stob a' Choire Odhair (Knoydart)		7
...	373	3134	Tom a' Chòinnich (Wyvis)		12
198	374	3133	Sgùrr nan Coireachan (Glenfinnan) ...		7
...	375	3132	Stob Coire Sgriodain (S. top) (Crags above Glac Bhàn)*		5
...	376	3130	A' Choinneach Mhòr *		10
199	377	3130	Buachaille Etive Bheag—Stob Dubh ...	[3129]	4
...	378	3130(ap.)	Meall nam Peithirean	[3000 cont.]	11
...	379	3129	Sgùrr nan Spainteach †		8
200	380	3128	Sgòr Gaibhre		5
...	381	3128	Druim Sgarsoch *		15
...	382	3128	Sròn Coire na h-Iolaire	[3125]	5
201	383	3125	Beinn Mhanach		3
202	384	3125	Sgùrr nan Coireachan (Glen Dessary) ...		7
...	385	3125(ap.)	Little Pap	[3000 cont.]	16

No. in order of Alt. Sep.Mt.	Top.	HEIGHT.	NAME.	Height, 1st edn.	Sect. in Table I.
203	386	3124	Sàileag		8
...	387	3121	Beinn Iutharn Bheag	[3011]	15
204	388	3120	Am Faochagach	...	15
...	389	3120	Stob na Bròige (Buachaille Etive Mòr)	...	12
205	390	3120	Meall Chuaich	...	4
206	391	3120(ap.)	Beinn Liath Mhòr (Fannaich) ...	[Prob. 3200]	15
...	392	3120(ap.)	Beinn Fhada (Glencoe) (Centre top)		11
207	393	3118	Meall Dearg (Aonach Eagach)	...	4
...	394	3110(ap.)	Beinn nan Eachan (E. top)	...	5
208	395	3109	Meall Gorm (N.W. top)	...	3
209	396	3107	Meall Buidhe (Knoydart) ...	...	11
210	397	3107	Sgùrr Mhic Coinnich ‡ ...	...	7
211	398	3106	Beinn Buidhe	...	17
...	399	3106	An Cabar (Wyvis)	...	1
212	400	3105	Driesh	...	12
...	401	3104	Sgùrr Squmain	...	16
...	402	3104	Sgòrr Bhan† (B. a' Bheithir) ...	...	17
213	403	3104	Beinn a' Chroin (E. top) ...	...	4
...	404	3104	Sgùrr na Banachdich (Centre top)‡	[3101]	1
...	405	3102	Creag Dhubh (Glen Cannich) ...	...	17
214	406	3102	Bidein a' Choire Sheasgaich ...	...	9
215	407	3102	Creag a' Mhàim	...	9
...	408	3101	Sgùrr a' Mhaoraich Beag * ...	...	7
...	409	3100(ap.)	Sgùrr na Forcan †	...	7
...	410	3100 „	Garbh Chìoch Bheag * ...	...	7
...	411	3100 „	Sgùrr a' Dubh Doire † ...	[3000 cont.]	8
...	412	3100 „	Sàil Liath ‡ (An Teallach) ...	...	11
...	413	3100 „	Sgùrr na Creige	[3000 cont.]	7
...	414	3100 „	Creag Leachdach	[3000 cont.]	16
...	415	3100 „	Creag an Dubh-loch	...	16
216	416	3099	Beinn Tulaichean	...	1
217	417	3098	Càrn Bhac (N.E. top) (Top of Coire Bhearnaist) ...		15
218	418	3098	Sgùrr na Sgine	...	7
219	419	3093	Càrn Dearg (N.W. top) (Monadh Liadth) ...	...	6
220	420	3092	Ben Vorlich (S. top) (Loch Lomond) ...	...	1
...	421	3089	[Stob] Coire nan Dearcag ...	...	8
221	422	3089	Sgùrr Dubh Mòr	[3110 ap.]	17
222	423	3087	Càrn Cloich-mhuilinn		14
223	424	3087	Càrn na Caim	...	15
224	425	3087	Càrn Bàn (Monadh Liadth) ...	...	6
...	426	3085	Am Bodach * (Aonach Eagach) ...	...	5
225	427	3084	Carn Dearg (Loch Ossian) ...	...	5
226	428	3083	Luinne Bheinn	...	7
...	429	3083	Stob a' Bhruaich Lèith (Stob Ghabhar)	...	4
227	430	3083	Binnein Beag	...	5
...	431	3082	Spidean Dhomhnuill Bhric ...	...	7
...	432	3080	Stob Coire Lèith * (Aonach Eagach)	...	5
...	433	3080(ap.)	Glas Mheall Liath * (An Teallach) ...		11
...	434	[3080 „	Beinn Tarsuinn] ‡		11
228	435	3078	Beinn a' Chroin (W. top) ...	...	1
229	436	3077	Mullach nan Coirean (N.W. top) ...	...	5
...	437	3077	Mount Keen	...	16
...	438	3077(ap.)	Glas Leathad Beag * (Centre Top)	[3000 cont.]	12
...	439	3075	East Meur. Gorm Craig ...	...	14
230	440	3074	Beinn Cheathaich	...	3
...	441	3073	An Sòcach (Sòcach Mòr) (Aberdeenshire) ...		15
231	442	3069	Sgùrr Dubh na Da Bheinn ...	[3080 ap.]	17
232	443	3066	Beinn na Lap	...	5
...	444	3066	Sròn a' Choire Ghairbh ...	...	7
233	445	3065	Stob Coire Altruim † (Buachaille Etive Mòr)	...	4
...	446	3064	A' Bhuidheanach Bheag (Drumochter) ...		15
...	447	3064	Beinn Fhada (N.E. top), (Bidean nam Bian)		4
234	448	3063	Ceann Garbh * (Meall nan Ceapraichean) ...	...	12
235	449	3062	Meall a' Chrasgaidh	...	11
236	450	3060	Maol Chean-dearg (Loch Carron) ...	...	10
237	451	3060	Fionn Bheinn	...	11
...	452	3060(ap.)	A' Mhaighdean	[3100 ap.]	11
238	453	3059	An Sòcach (W. end) (Aberdeenshire)	...	15
239	454	3059	The Cairnwell	...	15
...	455	3059	Beinn Sgulaird	[3058]	4
240	456	3058	Sgùrr an Tuill Bhàin (Slioch) ...	...	11
...	457	3058	Stob a' Choire Odhair (Black Mount)	...	4
...	458	3055	Creag a' Choir' Aird * (E. top)	...	8
...	459	3055(ap.)	Ben Vorlich (N. top), (Loch Lomond)		1
241	460	3054	Am Bàthaich	[3000 cont.]	7
242	461	3053	Meall Buidhe (Garbh Mheall) (Rannoch) ...	...	3
243	462	3051	Beinn Chabhair	...	1
...	463	3050(ap.)	Beinn Bhreac (E. top) ...	...	14
244	464	3050(ap.)	Am Fasarinen * (Liathach) ...	...	10
			Sgiath Chùil	...	3

Table II. Arranged in Order of Altitude. 49

No. in order of Alt. Sep.Mt.	Top.	HEIGHT.	NAME.	Height, 1st edn.	Sect. in Table I.
...	465	3050(ap.)	Corrag Bhuidhe Buttress † ‡ (An Teallach) ...		11
...	466	3050 „	Creag Dubh (B. Eighe)	[3000 cont.]	10
245	467	3050 „	Meall na Teanga		7
...	468	3050 „	A' Chìoch (L. Cluanie)	[3000 cont.]	8
246	469	3050 „	Am Bàsteir (Sgùrr Dubh a' Bhasteir)	[3020 ap.]	17
...	470	3050 „	Stùc a' Choire Dhuibh Bhig	[3000 ap.]	10
...	471	3050 „	Beinn Gharbh	[3000 cont.]	15
...	472	3050 „	Sgùrr a' Fionn Choire † ‡		17
...	473	3049	Meall Cruidh * (Ben Starav)		4
247	474	3048	Ben Chonzie		2
...	475	3045	Tigh Mòr na Seilge (N.N.E. top) ...		8
248	476	3045	A' Chailleach (Monadh Liadh) ...		6
...	477	3045(ap.)	Beinn Bhreac (W. top)	[3000 cont.]	14
249	478	3043	Mayar		16
250	479	3042	Blaven (Skye)		17
...	480	3041	Uinneag a Ghlas-Choire *		5
251	481	3041	Seana Bhraigh		12
...	482	3040	Sgòr Choinnich		5
...	483	3040(ap.)	[Stob] Cadha Gobhlach † (An Teallach)		11
252	484	3040	Ben Hope		13
...	485	3039	Ben Sgriol (N.W. top)	[3034]	7
253	486	3039	Eididh nan Clach Geala		12
254	487	3039	Meall nan Eun		4
...	488	3037	Glas Mheall Mòr (Drumochter) ...		15
255	489	3037	Sgùrr nan Eag (Cuillins)	[3036]	17
256	490	3036	Beinn Narnain		1
257	491	3036	Geal Chàrn (Monadh Liadh)		6
...	492	3035(ap.)	Meall Luaidhe * (Càrn Mairg)	[3000 cont.]	3
258	493	3034	Beinn Liath Mhòr		10
259	494	3033	Moruisg		9
260	495	3033	Meall a' Choire Lèith		3
...	496	3031	Sròn Chona Choirein		3
261	497	3031	Creag Pitridh		5
...	498	3030(ap.)	Meall Gorm (S.E. top)	[3000 cont.]	11
...	499	3029	Stob Coire Raineach * (Buachaille Etive Bheag) ...		4
...	500	3029	Diollaid a' Chàirn		5
...	501	3027	Craig of Gowal		16
...	502	3027(ap.)	Glas Leathad Beag * (W. top)	[3000 cont.]	12
262	503	3026	Sgùrr nan Each		11
...	504	3025	Càrn Dearg (S.E. top) (Monadh Liadth) ...		6
...	505	3025	Mullach Coire nan Nead *		5
...	506	3025(ap.)	Sàil Chaoruinn	[3000 cont.]	8
...	507	3021	Tom na Gruagaich (B. Alligin) ...		10
263	508	3021	Beinn an Lochain (Glencroe)		1
...	509	3020	Beinn a Chùirn		3
264	510	3020(ap.)	Càrn Ballach (N.E. top)	[3000 cont.]	6
265	511	3019	Geal Chàrn (Glenfeshie)		14
...	512	3019	Meall Odhar		16
...	513	3018	Fiachlach (Wyvis)		12
266	514	3017	An Socach * (Glen Affric)		8
267	515	3015	Gairich		7
268	516	3015	Càrn Sgùlain		6
269	517	3015	An Coileachan		11
...	518	3015(ap.)	Tom na Sròine *	[3000 cont.]	5
...	519	3014	Crow Craigies *		16
...	520	3014	Càrn Bhac (S.W. top)		15
270	521	3014	Sgùrr a' Mhadaidh ‡ (S.W. peak) (2 tops) ...		17
...	522	3013	Sgùrr Leac nan Each		7
271	523	3012	Creag nan Damh		7
...	524	3011	Snechdach Slinnean * (Monadh Liadth) ...		6
...	525	3010(ap.)	Faochag	[3000 cont.]	7
...	526	3009	[Stob] Lochan nan Cnapan		14
272	527	3008	Beinn a' Chleibh		1
...	528	3007	Meall a' Churain		3
...	529	3007	Sgùrr Thormaid * † (Cuillins) ...		17
...	530	3006	[Stob] Coire Lochan (Càrn Eige) ...		8
273	531	3006	A' Ghlas-bheinn (L. Duich)		8
...	532	3006	Càrn Bhinnein		15
274	533	3005	Geal Chàrn (L. Ericht)		5
...	534	3004	Meall Buidhe (S.E. top)		3
275	535	3004	Ben Vane		1
...	536	3004	Mullach nan Coirean (S.E. top) ...		5
...	537	3004	Meall Cuanail (Cruachan)		4
...	538	3004	Meall a' Chaoruinn		15
276	539	3003	Càrn Aosda		15
...	540	3002	[Stob] Choire Dhuibh (Creag Meaghaidh) ...		6
...	541	3002	An Sgòr *		3
...	542	3000	Càrn nan Sac		15
...	543	3000(ap.)	Bhàster Tooth † ‡		17
...	544	[3000 cont.	Càrn a' Bhutha.] ‡ §		15

§ with Beinn Tarsuinn, 277 and 545

ADDITIONAL NOTES.

THE following notes collate data regarding Munro's Tables available to the Editor from the following sources: footnotes to the 1933 edition of the Tables; S.M.C. Journals and Guidebooks; notebooks of, and correspondence from, members of the Club. They have been set out in this form for easy reference, so that all information regarding the height, etc., of each top named is shown at a glance.

Section 3.

CÀRN MAIRG:

Meall a' Bhàrr: 3300 ap. J.G.S.

Creag Mhòr: 3200 J.G.S.; 3240 (N.E. top) J.G.I.; well marked W. top ½m W.S.W. 3190 J.G.I.

Meall Garbh: 3233 (W. top) J.G.I.; other tops ¼ m. E. (3220 ap.) and ½ m. S.E. (3160 ap.); both fairly well marked.

LAWERS RANGE:

Beinn Ghlas: 3645 F.S.G.; 3624 J.G.I.; 3623 J.R.C.

Meall Corranaich: 3494 F.S.G.; 3529 J.R.C.

TARMACHAN RANGE:

Meall Garbh: 3400 H.T.M.; 3350 A.W.R.; 3365 J.G.I.; 3370 R.G.I.

Beinn nan Eachan, W.: 3290 J.G.I.; 3300 R.G.I.

Beinn nan Eachan, E.: 3100 R.G.I.

SGIATH CHÙIL: 3030 R.B.; 3035 J.G.I.; 3025 R.G.I.

Section 5.

AN GEARANACH: 3240 J.G.I.; 3250 R.G.I.

AN GARBHANACH: 3230 J.G.I.; 3240 R.G.I.

SGÙRR A' MHAIM:

Sgòr an Iubhair: 3300 R.G.I.

Stob a' Coire Mhail: another prominent top, 3250 cont. ½ m. S. of Sg. a' Mhaim, with 175-200 ft. dip on each side; 3300 ap. R.G.I.

BEN NEVIS, CÀRN DEARG N.W.: actual top on edge of cliff, some 300 yds. S. of O.S. cairn. J.G.I.; Agreed; at top of N. Trident Buttress, R.G.I.; 4020 J.G.I.; 3990, mean of several observations, R.G.I.

AONACH MÒR:

Stob an Cul Choire: 3530 E.M.C.; 3540 R.G.I.

Stob Co. an Fhir Duibhe: 3325 J.D.; 3295 R.G.I.

Tom na Sròine: 3010 R.G.I.

CLAURIGHS:

Stob Co. Claurigh, N.: 3660 J.G.I.

Stob Co. Gaibhre: 3080 H.T.M.; 3172 E.M.C.; 3095 J.G.I.

Stob Co. Ceannain: 3657 E.M.C.

BEINN A' CHLACHAIR: important N.E. Top 3138 R.B.

SGAIRNEACH MHÒR: 3260 J.G.I.; agreed, on two occasions, R.G.I.

Section 7.

MEALL NA TEANGA: 3012 E.M.C.; 3000 J.R.C., R.G.I.

GARBH CHIÒCH MÒR: 3315 E.W. Hodge.

GARBH CHIÒCH BEAG: 3160 E.W. Hodge.

Section 7—Contd.

SADDLE, SGÙRR NA FORCAN: 3050 E.M.C.; 3100 A.E.R.

SGURR A' MHAORAICH: Gurr Thionail, 1½m. N. of 3365 pt., 2965 ft., looks higher than Am Bàthaich; 3065 ap. R.B., J.R.C.

Section 8.

SGÙRR NAN CEATHREAMHNAN: another prominent top, 3000 ft. cont. ⅝ m. N. by W. of Stùc Mòr.

BEINN FHADA:
Ceum na h-Aon Choise: 3160 H.T.M.

CREAG A' CHOIR' AIRD, S. top (1933 edn., " Southern Ridge "): 3215 J.D.; 3190 J.R.C.; the adverse comment on the inference drawn from the hill shading has been deleted from the note in the 1933 edn., as it does not apply to the position " ½ m. S. of the 3188 ft. top ". The " 1½ m. S." of the 1921 edn. seems to have been a clerical error, as H.T.M.'s card index has " ½ m. S.", agreeing with J.D.'s position, and height of 3215 ft.

TOM A' CHOINICH BEAG: 3325 H.T.M.; 3460 E.M.C.; 3463 L.H.; 3375 J.R.C.; certainly 50 ft. lower than An Leth-Chreag, J.D.; in view of several readings about 3450 ft., it seems possible that the O.S. height of An Leth-Chreag may not be that of the actual top.

Section 9.

SGÙRR NA LÀPAICH:
Rudha na Spreidhe: 3453 R.B.; 3443 L.H.
Sgùrr nan Clachan Geala: 3573 R.B.; fully 3500 C.P.
Creag a' Chaoruinn: 3183 R.B.

AN RIABHACHAN: The hill shading, on which the 3730 ft. estimate of the 1921 edn. was based, having been found erroneous, and the confirming 3700 ft. contour now stated to be only approximate, the height of 3696 ft. in the 1st edn. has been restored. The county Boundary top is not more than 10 ft. lower, there being a point 3686 close to the boundary.

Section 10.

LIATHACH:
Bidean Toll a' Mhuic: 3250 H.T.M.; 3210 J.R.C.
Stùc a' Choire Duibhe Bhig: well over 3000 L.H.; 3001 R.B.; 2950 J.R.C.
Meall Dearg: 3040 J.R.C.
Am Fasarinen: 2940 J.R.C.

BEINN EIGHE:
A' Choinneach Mhòr: 3170 J.R.C.; 3150 R.G.I.
Spidean Coire nan Clach: 3275 R.B.; 3250 R.G.I.
Creag Dubh: 3050 R.G.I.

Section 11.

BEINN TARSUINN: 2850 ft. Contour, 6¾ m. N. of Kinlochewe; 2980 C.P.;
3080 J.R.C., J.G.I., J.A.P., and many others; 3075 ft., and photo
of B. Eighe shows it is not lower than Sg. an Tuill Bhain: Mr J.
Hirst. The status of this hill seems well established. *Note by
Mr. Colin Philip:* " The map of this part was very casual; I think
the O.S. had bad weather, and were hurried in order to meet the
views of the then laird."

SLIOCH: See Mr J. A. Parker's article: *S.M.C.J.* Vol. 20, p. 402: " the
whole matter had been investigated, and the (3250 ft.) contour
would be deleted." *Director General, O.S.*

A' MHAIGHDEAN: 3140 R.B.

MULLACH COIRE MHIC FHEARCHAIR: a well marked S.E. top, Tom
Coinnich, noted, R.B., J.G.I.; 3229 ap. R.B.; 3166 J.R.C.; 3150
estimate, J.G.I.

AN TEALLACH:
Glas Meall Liath: 3130 H.T.M.
Sgùrr Creag an Eich: 3380 H.T.M.
Lord Berkeley's Seat: 3325 W.D.; 3375 R.B.
Corrag Bhuidhe: 3425 H.T.M.; 3315 R.B.
Cadha Gobhlach: 3100 H.T.M.; 3040 R.B.
Sàil Liath: 3020 R.B.

FANNAICHS:
Sgùrr Breac: 3286 R.B.
Meall nam Peithirean: 3140 E.M.C.; 3097 R.B.; 3145 R.G.I.
Beinn Liath Mhor Fannaich: 3250 E.M.C.; 3137 R.B.
Meall Gorm, S.E. top: 3042 R.B.
Tom Coinnich: top of Druim Reidh Ridge, 1 m. E. of A' Chailleach,
2750 cont.; 3131 ap. R.B.; certainly over 3000 ft. but not so high
as R.B.'s figures. J.R.C.

Section 12.

BEN WYVIS:
Glas Leathad Beag, Centre top: 3030 H.T.M.

MEALL NAN CEAPRÀICHEAN: 3175 J.G.I. 3192 R.B.; the top is at the S.
end of the ridge, where the O.S. has only a 3100 contour. The
3150 contour to the north is only an undulation in a rising ridge,
some 25 ft. lower than the actual top.

CONA' MHEALL: 3225 J.G.I.

CÀRN GORM LOCH: 2950 cont. 1¼ m. E. of Am Faochagach, 2990 J.R.C.,
R.G.I.; 3010 R.B.; over 3000, note H.T.M.

Section 13.

FOINAVEN: 2980 ft.; 3013 ft. ap. R.B. (see *S.M.C.J.* xv. 339); under
3000 J.R.C.

BEN MORE ASSYNT, S. top: 3150 J. Nicholson.

Section 14.

BEINN BHREAC, W. top: 3043 R.B.

BYNACK MORE: R.B. and J.R.C. draw attention to Bynack Beag, 3200 ft.
cont.; 3194 R.B.

CAIRNTOUL:
Angels' Peak: 4116 J. Y. McDonald.

BEINN BHROTAIN: well marked top ⅝ m. E. 3550 ap. E.M.C.

MONADH MÒR: another top ¾ m. S.E. by S., 3575 ap. E.M.C.

Section 15.

CÀRN BHÀC, S.W. top: this should be " Centre Top "; the real S.W.
top is Càrn a' Bhutha.

CÀRN BHÀC:
Càrn a' Bhutha: Extract from letters from O.S. Office, Southampton:
" There is no instrumental height recorded on the original 6 in.
On the original hill sketching a figure of 3000 ft. is recorded, probably referring to the summit as the estimated height, as the 3000 ft.
contour is not penned in, implying that the peak reaches 3000 ft.
and no more." See *S.M.C.J.* xx. 285.

Section 16.

CAIRN BANNOCH:
Creag Leachdach: 3150 H.T.M., R.B.

LOCHNAGAR:
Little Pap: 3137 J.G.I.; 3130 R.G.I.

Section 17.

(See S.M.C. Guidebook (G.B.) and *S.M.C.J.* xvi. 244-249).

SKYE:
Am Bàsteir: 3070 G.B.; 3020 J.N.C.
Sgùrr a' Fionn Choire: 3065 G.B.
Sgùrr a' Mhadaidh, S.W. top: 3010 G.B.
Sgùrr a' Ghreadaidh, N. top: 3190 G.B.; 3100 J.N.C.
Sgùrr Thormaid: 3040 G.B.
Sgùrr na Banachdich, Centre top: 3090 G.B.
Sgùrr Dearg, Cairn: 3206 G.B.
Inaccessible Pinnacle: 3226 G.B.; 3250 J.N.C.
Sgùrr Alasdair: 3251 G.B.; 3255 J.N.C.
Sgùrr Thearlaich: 3201 G.B.; 3210 J.N.C.
Sgùrr Dubh Mòr: 3110 J.N.C.
Sgùrr Dubh na Da Bheinn: 3080 J.N.C.

INDEX TO TABLE I., MUNRO'S TABLES.

Names in italic indicate the locality, or the " separate mt." to which the top belongs. To facilitate reference, in long Sections, ¼, ½, etc., has been added to the Section number to indicate roughly the whereabouts of the name. Thus 7¼ means from about a quarter nearly half way through the Section; 7½, half to nearly threequarters way through; and 7¾ from nearly three-quarters way to the end. Different spellings in the 1st edition are marked *.

A' ; Am; An; Ben, Beinn; Càrn; Creag; Meall; Sgòr, Sgàrr; Sròn; Stob; see next word.

A' ; Am; An; Ben, Beinn; Càrn; Creag; Meall; Sgòr, Sgàrr; Sròn; Stob; see next word.

56 *Index to Table I., Munro's Tables.*

C.I.C. hut and north face buttresses of Ben Nevis.

Ben Ime.

2

Corbett's Tables

SCOTTISH MOUNTAINS 2500 FEET AND UNDER 3000 FEET IN HEIGHT
WITH RE-ASCENT OF 500 FEET ON ALL SIDES

by J. ROOKE CORBETT

FOREWORD

by John Dow

J. ROOKE CORBETT did not publish his List of 2,500-foot mountains, all of which he himself had ascended, probably because he felt that before doing so some further checking on the ground would be desirable. After his death it was passed by his sister to the Guide Books General Editor, who decided that it was worthy of record as of interest and assistance to hill walkers generally, and it has been printed as he left it subject to some minor amendments in the column headed " Position".

There was no indication in Corbett's papers as to the criterion he adopted in listing the heights included, but it seems clear that his only test was a re-ascent of 500 feet on all sides to every point admitted, no account being taken of distance or difficulty. No detailed check has been made, but the 500 feet qualification has obviously been exhaustively applied and rigidly adhered to; Sgùrr na Ba Glaise (2,817) in Section 7 has been suggested as a possible omission if the map contours are correct, whilst the two hills of equal height (2,658) in Section 6, which are $2\frac{1}{4}$ miles apart and divided only by about 350 feet of dip, were probably included as joint claimants.

The List is accordingly not strictly comparable with those compiled by either Munro or Donald as it does not profess to include all " summits " and " tops " from 2,500 to 2,999 feet, which on a Munro basis would give a much larger total.

SCOTTISH MOUNTAINS 2500 FEET

AND UNDER 3000 FEET IN HEIGHT

WITH RE-ASCENT OF 500 FEET ON ALL SIDES

Name	Height	4 figure map ref.		1-in. O.S. 7th Ed.
SECTION 1A. *South of the Forth-Clyde Canal.*				
Merrick	2,765	42	85	73
Kirriereoch Hill	2,565	41	87	,,
Shalloch on Minnoch	2,520	40	90	,,
Corserine	2,669	49	87	,,
Cairnsmore of Carsphairn . . .	2,613	59	98	67
Hart Fell	2,651	11	13	69
Broad Law	2,754	14	23	,,
Cramalt Craig	2,723	17	25	,,
White Coomb	2,695	16	15	,,
SECTION 1B. *West of Loch Lomond.*				
Beinn Chuirn	2,878	28	29	53
Meall an Fhudair	2,508	27	19	,,
Binnein an Fhidleir	2,680	21	10	,,
Beinn Luibhean	2,811	24	07	,,
Ben Arthur (The Cobbler) . . .	2,891	25	05	,,
Ben Donich	2,774	21	04	,,
The Brack	2,580	24	03	,,
Beinn Bheula	2,557	15	98	,,
SECTION 1C. *East of Loch Lomond.*				
Beinn a' Choin	2,524	35	13	53
Stob a' Choin	2,839	41	16	,,
Ceann na Baintighearna . . .	2,526	47	16	54
Creag Mac Ranaich . . .	2,600+	54	25	,,
Meall an t'Seallaidh . . .	2,793	54	23	,,
Ben Vane	2,685	53	13	,,
Ben Ledi	2,873	56	09	,,
SECTION 2.				
Creag Uchdag	2,887	70	32	48
Creagan na Beinne . . .	2,909	74	36	,,
Auchnafree Hill	2,565	81	30	,,
Meall na Fearna	2,500+	65	18	54

Name	Height	4 figure map ref.	1-in. O.S. 7th Ed.
SECTION 3.			
Meall Buidhe	2,976	42 45	47
Cam Chreag	2,823	53 49	48
Beinn Dearg	2,702	60 49	,,
Meall nan Tairneachan	2,559	80 54	,,
Farragon Hill	2,559	84 55	,,
Meall nan Subh	2,638	46 39	47
Beinn an Oighreag	2,978	54 41	48
Meall Luaidhe	2,558	58 43	,,
Beinn Udlaidh	2,759	28 33	47
Beinn Bhreac-Liath	2,633	30 34	,,
Beinn nam Fuaran	2,632	36 38	,,
Beinn a' Chaisteal	2,897	34 36	,,
Beinn Odhar	2,948	33 33	,,
Beinn Chaorach	2,655	36 32	,,
Beinn nan Imirean	2,769	42 31	,,
SECTION 4.			
Fraochaidh	2,883	02 51	46
Beinn Maol Chaluim	2,967	13 52	47
Creach Bheinn	2,657	02 42	46
Beinn Trilleachan	2,752	08 44	,,
Stob Dubh, Beinn Ceitlin . . .	2,897	16 48	47
Beinn Mhic Chasgaig	2,820	22 50	,,
Beinn Mhic Mhonaidh	2,602	21 35	,,
Beinn a' Bhuiridh	2,941	09 28	53
SECTION 5A. *West of Tyndrum—Fort William Railway*			
Cruach Innse	2,850+	28 76	36
Sgùrr Innse	2,600+	29 74	47
Mam na Gualainn	2,603	11 62	46
Glas Bheinn	2,587	26 64	47
Leum Uilleim	2,971	33 64	,,
Garbh Bheinn	2,835	17 60	,,
Beinn a' Chrulaiste	2,805	24 56	,,
SECTION 5B. *East of Tyndrum—Fort William Railway*			
The Fara	2,986	59 84	37
Beinn Chumhain	2,958	46 71	47
Stob an Aonaich Mhoir . . .	2,805	53 69	48
Meall na Leitreach	2,544	64 70	,,
Beinn Mholach	2,758	58 65	,,
Beinn a' Chuallaich	2,925	68 61	,,

Name	Height	4 figure map ref.	1-in. O.S. 7th Ed.
SECTION 6.			
Beinn Teallach	2,994	36 86	36
Carn Dearg, Glen Roy	2,736	34 88	,,
Beinn Iaruinn	2,636	29 90	,,
Carn Dearg	2,523	35 94	,,
Carn Dearg	2,677	35 96	,,
Gairbeinn	2,929	46 98	,,
Meall na h'Aisre	2,825	51 00	,,
Carn Chuilinn	2,677	41 03	,,
Carn Fasgann Bana	2,554	48 06	,,
Carn na Laraiche Maoile . . .	2,658	58 11	37
Carn na Saobhaidhe	2,658	60 14	,,
Carn an Fhreiceadain	2,879	72 07	,,
Geal-Charn Mor	2,702	83 12	,,
SECTION 7A. *South of Loch Eil and Loch Shiel.*			
Ben Resipol	2,774	76 65	46
Sgùrr Dhomhnuill.	2,915	89 68	,,
Druim Garbh	2,637	88 68	,,
Carn na Nathrach	2,579	88 70	,,
Druim Tarsuinn	2,520	87 . 72	
Sgùrr Ghiubhsachain	2,784	87 75	35
Sgor Craobh a' Chaoruinn . . .	2,543	89 75	,,
Stob Coire a' Chearcaill . . .	2,527	01 72	46
Garbh Bheinn	2,903	90 62	,,
Creach Bheinn	2,800	87 57	,,
Fuar Bheinn	2,511	85 56	,,
SECTION 7B. *Between Loch Shiel and the Mallaig Railway*			
Roisbheinn	2,887	75 77	35
An Stac	2,550	76 79	,,
Druim Fiaclach	2,852	79 79	,,
Beinn Odhar Bheag	2,895	84 78	,,
SECTION 7C. *North of Mallaig Railway and South of Loch Nevis, Loch Quoich and Glen Garry.*			
Ben Aden	2,905	89 98	35
Sgùrr na h'Aide	2,818	88 93	,,
Carn Mor	2,718	90 91	,,
Sgùrr an Fhuarain.	2,961	98 98	,,
Fraoch Bheinn	2,808	98 94	,,

Name	Height	4 figure map ref.		1-in. O.S. 7th Ed.
Sgùrr Mhurlagain	2,885	01	94	35
Geal Charn	2,636	15	94	36
Meall Coire nan Saobhaidh . . .	2,695	17	95	,,
Ben Tee	2,957	24	97	,,
Beinn Bhan	2,613	14	85	35
Meall a' Phubuill	2,533	03	85	,,
Braigh na h'Uamhachan . . .	2,513	97	86	,,
Streap	2,988	94	86	,,
Beinn an Tuim	2,656	93	83	,,
Sgùrr nan Utha	2,610	88	84	,,

SECTION 7D.
North of Loch Nevis, Loch Quoich and Glen Garry

Name	Height	4 figure map ref.		1-in. O.S. 7th Ed.
Sgùrr Mhic Bharraich	2,553	91	17	35
Beinn na h'Eaglaise	2,650+	85	12	,,
Beinn na Caorach	2,536	87	12	,,
Buidhe Bheinn	2,900+	95	08	,,
Beinn na Caillich	2,573	79	06	,,
Sgùrr Coire Choinnichean . . .	2,612	79	01	,,
Beinn Bhuidhe	2,803	82	96	,,
Sgùrr a' Choire-Bheithe . . .	2,994	89	01	,,
Sgùrr nan Eugallt	2,933	93	04	,,
Druim nan Cnamh	2,555	13	07	,,
Meall Dubh	2,581	24	08	36

SECTION 8.

Name	Height	4 figure map ref.		1-in. O.S. 7th Ed.
Sgùrr an Airgid	2,757	94	22	26
Am Bathach	2,605	07	14	35
Carn a' Choire Ghairbh . . .	2,827	13	19	,,
Aonach Shasuinn	2,901	17	18	36

SECTION 9.

Name	Height	4 figure map ref.		1-in. O.S. 7th Ed.
Sgùrr a' Mhuillin	2,845	26	55	27
Meallan nan Uan	2,750+	26	54	,,
Bac an Eich	2,791	22	49	,,
An Sithean	2,661	17	45	,,
Sgùrr nan Ceannaichean . . .	2,986	08	48	26
Sgùrr na Feartaig	2,830	05	45	,,
Beinn Tharsuinn	2,807	05	43	,,
Beinn Dronaig	2,612	03	38	,,
Sguman Coinntich	2,881	97	30	,,
Faochaig	2,847	02	31	,,
Aonach Buidhe	2,949	05	32	,,
Sgùrr na Diollaid	2,676	28	36	27
Beinn a' Bhalach Ard . . .	2,826	36	43	,,

Name	Height	4 figure map ref.		1-in. O.S. 7th Ed.

SECTION 10.

Name	Height	4 figure map ref.		1-in. O.S. 7th Ed.
Baosbheinn	2,869	87	65	19
Beinn an Eoin	2,801	90	64	26
Beinn Dearg	2,995	89	60	,,
Meall a' Ghuibhais . . .	2,882	97	63	,,
Ruadh-Stac Beag	2,850+	97	61	,,
Sgùrr Dubh	2,566	97	55	,,
Sgorr nan Lochan Uaine . .	2,840	96	53	,,
Fuar Tholl	2,968	97	49	,,
An Ruadh Stac	2,919	92	48	,,
Beinn Damh	2,957	89	50	,,
Beinn Bhan	2,936	80	44	,,
Sgùrr a' Chaorachain . . .	2,600	79	41	,,

SECTION 11.

Name	Height	4 figure map ref.		1-in. O.S. 7th Ed.
Beinn Airidh Charr . . .	2,593	93	76	19
Beinn Lair	2,817	98	73	19 and 20
Beinn a' Chaisgein Mor . .	2,802	98	78	,, ,,
Ruadh-Stac Mor	2,850+	02	75	,, ,,
Creag Rainich	2,646	09	75	,, ,,
Beinn a' Chlaidheimh . . .	2,960+	06	77	,, ,,
Beinn Dearg Mhor . . .	2,974	03	80	,, ,,
Beinn Dearg Bheag . . .	2,550+	02	81	,, ,,
Sail Mhor, An Teallach . .	2,508	03	88	,, ,,

SECTION 12.

Name	Height	4 figure map ref.		1-in. O.S. 7th Ed.
Beinn Enaiglair	2,915	22	80	20
Beinn a' Chaisteal . . .	2,580	37	80	21
Carn Ban	2,762	33	87	20
Carn Chuinneag	2,749	48	83	21

SECTION 13.

Name	Height	4 figure map ref.		1-in. O.S. 7th Ed.
Cul Beag	2,523	14	08	13 and 20
Cul Mor	2,786	16	11	13
Canisp	2,779	20	18	,,
Creag Liath, Breabag . . .	2,670	28	15	,,
Glas Bheinn	2,541	25	26	,,
Spidean Coinich . . .	2,508	20	27	,,
Sail Gharbh, Quinag . . .	2,653	21	29	,,
Beinn Leoid	2,597	32	29	,,
Ben Hee	2,864	42	34	14

Name	Height	4 figure map ref.		1-in. O.S. 7th Ed.
Meallan Liath Coire Mhic Dhugaill .	2,625	35	39	14
Meall Horn	2,548	35	44	9
Arkle	2,580	31	45	,,
Ganu Mor, Foinaven . . .	2,980	31	50	,,
Cranstackie	2,630	35	55	,,
Beinn Spionnaidh	2,537	36	57	,,
Ben Loyal	2,504	57	48	10

SECTION 14.

Name	Height	4 figure map ref.		1-in. O.S. 7th Ed.
Sgor Mor	2,666	00	91	38 and 41
Carn na Drochaide . . .	2,681	12	93	,, ,,
Creag an Dail Bheag . . .	2,830	15	98	,, ,,
Cularloch	2,953	19	98	,, ,,
Brown Cow Hill	2,721	22	04	,, ,,
Morven	2,862	37	04	39 and 42
Creag Mhor	2,932	05	04	38 and 41
Meall a' Bhuachaille . . .	2,654	99	11	,, ,,
Geal Charn	2,692	09	12	,, ,,
Carn Ealasaid	2,600	22	11	,, ,,
Carn Mor	2,636	26	18	,, 39
Cook's Cairn	2,541	30	27	,, ,,
Corriehabbie	2,563	28	28	,, ,,
Ben Rinnes	2,755	25	35	29

SECTION 15.

Name	Height	4 figure map ref.		1-in. O.S. 7th Ed.
Meallach Mor	2,521	77	90	37
Carn Dearg Mor	2,813	82	91	,,
An Dun	2,707	71	80	,,
Craig an Loch	2,844	73	80	,,
Leathad an Taobhain . . .	2,994	81	85	,,
Beinn Bhreac	2,992	86	82	,,
Beinn Mheadhonach . . .	2,950 +	88	75	49
Ben Vrackie	2,757	95	63	41 and 49
Ben Vuirich	2,961	99	70	49
Meall Uaine	2,600	11	67	41 and 49
Ben Gulabin	2,641	10	72	41
Sgor Mor	2,908	11	82	,,
Morrone	2,819	13	88	

SECTION 16.

Name	Height	4 figure map ref.		1-in. O.S. 7th Ed.
Creag nan Gabhar	2,736	15	84	41
Monameanach	2,643	17	70	41 and 49
Conachraig	2,827	28	86	41 and 42

Name	Height	4 figure map ref.	1-in. O.S. 7th Ed.
Ben Tirran	2,939	37 74	42
Mount Battock	2,555	55 84	,,
SECTION 17. *Islands.*			
Harris—			
Clisham	2,622	15 07	12 and 18
Skye—			
Glamaig	2,537	51 30	25 and 33
Garbh-Bheinn	2,649	53 23	,, ,,
Rhum—			
Askival	2,659	39 95	33 and 34
Ainshval	2,552	37 94	,, ,,
Mull—			
Dun da Ghaoithe	2,512	67 36	45
Jura—			
Beinn an Oir	2,571	49 74	57
Arran—			
Goat Fell	2,866	99 41	59 and 66
Beinn Tarsuinn	2,706	96 41	,, ,,
Cir Mhor	2,618	97 43	,, ,,
Caisteal Abhail	2,817	96 44	,, ,,

Strath na Sheallag (Ross-shire) and Beinn Dearg Mor.

Ben Lomond, Summit Ridge.

3

Donald's Tables

ALL HILLS IN THE SCOTTISH LOWLANDS
2000 FEET IN HEIGHT AND ABOVE

by PERCY DONALD, B.Sc.

INTRODUCTION

IN the preparation of the following tables, free use has been made of both the popular* and hill-shaded editions of the 1-inch O.S. map and of the 6-inch O.S. map. In addition, every elevation of 2,000 feet or over has been visited at least once, and many of the points examined were discarded as unworthy of inclusion as "tops". The method of determining "hills" and "tops" is described later, but it may be mentioned here that the definite policy was adopted of excluding from the list of "tops" all points of doubtful merit.

The total number of hills is 86 and of tops 133. The most northerly hill is Innerdownie in the Ochils, the most easterly Windy Gyle in the Cheviots (or Auchope Cairn on The Cheviot if tops are considered),** the most southerly Cairnsmore of Fleet, and the most westerly Shalloch on Minnoch, both in Galloway. (Extreme points in the last two cases are actually tops, *i.e.*, Knee of Cairnsmore and Shalloch on Minnoch, North Top.)

The highest hills and elevations in each county are given in the following list:—

		Feet
Kirkcudbright	Merrick	2,764
Peebles and Selkirk	Broad Law	2,754
Dumfries	White Coomb	2,695
Peebles	Dollar Law	2,680
Ayr and Kirkcudbright	Ord. Pt. on Kirriereoch Hill	2,565
Ayr	Shalloch on Minnoch	2,528
Lanark and Peebles	Culter Fell	2,454

* Now the Seventh O.S. Series
** Cauldcleuch Head in Roxburgh is the most easterly hill wholly in Scotland.

			Feet
Roxburgh and Northumberland	.	Highest ground on Union Boundary	2,422
Lanark	.	Green Lowther . . .	2,403
Roxburgh and Northumberland	.	Top—Auchope Cairn . .	2,382
Clackmannan	.	Bencleuch	2,363
Midlothian	.	Blackhope Scar . . .	2,137
Selkirk	.	Top—Clockmore . . .	2,105 ap.
Roxburgh and Northumberland	.	Windy Gyle	2,034
Roxburgh	.	Cauldcleuch Head . . .	2,028

The allocation of hills and tops to counties is as follows:—

	Hills	Tops
Perth	1	1
Perth and Clackmannan	2	2
Clackmannan	2	6
Midlothian	1	1
Midlothian and Peebles	1	1
Peebles	15	26
Lanark and Peebles	3	4
Lanark	7	8
Peebles and Selkirk	7	9
Selkirk	...	2
Peebles and Dumfries	2	3
Dumfries	8	15
Dumfries and Selkirk	6	10
Dumfries and Lanark	5	6
Ayr and Dumfries	1	1
Ayr	4	6
Ayr and Kirkcudbright	1	2
Kirkcudbright	18	27
Roxburgh	1	1
Roxburgh and Northumberland	1	2
	86	133

Grouping by heights gives the following result:—

	Hills	Tops
From 2,764 to 2,700 inclusive	3	3
,, 2,699 ,, 2,600 ,, ...	6	9
,, 2,599 ,, 2,500 ,, ...	3	4
,, 2,499 ,, 2,400 ,, ...	7	10
,, 2,399 ,, 2,300 ,, ...	9	17
,, 2,299 ,, 2,200 ,, ...	23	28
,, 2,199 ,, 2,100 ,, ...	18	27
,, 2,099 ,, 2,000 ,, ...	17	35
	86	133

EXPLANATION OF TABLES

Table I

In this Table the following natural grouping has been adopted:—

Section	Area	Hills	Tops
1	Ochil Hills	5	9
2	Moorfoot Hills	5	5
3	Tinto	1	1
4	Enclosed by the Biggar-Broughton-Moffat roads .	5	8
5	Enclosed by the Broughton-Innerleithen-St Mary's Loch-Tweedsmuir roads . . .	13	20
6	Enclosed by the Tweedsmuir-St Mary's Loch-Moffat roads	10	21
7	Enclosed by the Moffat-St Mary's Loch-Tushielaw-Eskdalemuir roads	9	15
8	Between the Abington-Moffat and New Cumnock-Thornhill roads	12	15
9	Between the New Cumnock-Thornhill and Dalmellington-New Galloway roads	6	10
10	Between the Dalmellington-New Galloway Station and Girvan-Creetown roads	18	26
11	Cauldcleuch Head	1	1
12	Cheviot Hills (on Union Boundary) . . .	1	2
		86	133

Section 12 includes also five hills wholly in England.

An Appendix gives particulars of fifteen additional elevations not meriting inclusion as tops, but all enclosed by an isolated 2,000-feet contour. These have been included in order that the table may be a complete record of every separate area of ground reaching the 2,000-feet level.

Column 1—*Name.*—The Ordnance Survey spelling is always followed, a * implying that the name appears only on the 6-inch map. Where no name appears on either map the top has been given the name of its hill with N., S., etc., Top added. In all other cases the name is to be found on both the 6-inch and 1-inch maps. The number in this column is merely for convenience of reference from Tables II and III.

Column 2—Height.—The heights given fall into three main categories. (1) Heights given without qualification are the same on both the 6-inch and 1-inch O.S. maps. (2) Heights marked thus ° are from the 1-inch O.S. map, but there is close agreement with the values given on the 6-inch O.S. map. This category comprises cases where the 6-inch O.S. surface level is 1 foot higher or lower than the corresponding 1-inch O.S. height, where a Cr. level lies within the limits of 2 feet below and 1 foot above the 1-inch O.S. height, or where a B.M. level lies within the limits of 1 foot below or 2 feet above the 1-inch O.S. height. (3) Heights not shown on the 1-inch O.S. map are in every case preceded by the 1-inch O.S. height or contour height in parentheses. If there is no further qualification the height is a surface level from the 6-inch O.S. map. If based on a level other than a surface level on the 6-inch O.S. map a footnote gives particulars. If no level is given on any map the height is marked " ap." and is an approximate aneroid observation or an estimate made by the compiler. (An estimate is only used where the height difference required is too small to be accurately measured by aneroid.)

The following points are of interest in connection with the determination of hill heights and indicate the difficulties in the way of obtaining precise values.

The popular edition of the 1-inch O.S. gives heights in relation to assumed mean sea-level, while the 6-inch O.S. is still based on the assumed mean sea-level at Liverpool, which is 0·65 foot below mean sea-level.

Heights of hills on the O.S. maps are, in general, surface heights at triangulation points. Where such point is some distance from the top an approximate aneroid or estimated allowance can be made if no top height is given on the 6-inch O.S. Where such height is apparently at the top it would usually be impossible to locate its exact position relative to the top without information and possibly personal assistance from the Ordnance Survey Department. Consequently such heights may be a foot or two lower than the true top level.

In those cases where the 6-inch O.S. gives no surface level the First Edition Cr. level can be used as a rough guide. This level may be anything down to 18 inches below ground-level.   Failing both surface and Cr. levels a B.M. level can be used.   Such a level is often on the side of a fence-post about 2 feet above ground-level, but may be cut on a large boulder or on native rock surface.   Many of these B.M. marks have disappeared.

Column 3—*County.*—Tops less than $\frac{1}{16}$ mile from the county boundary are regarded as being in both counties.   In this column is also given the sheet-number of the 1-inch Seventh Edition O.S. map in which the top will be found.

Columns 4 *and* 5—*Hill No. and Top No.*—These give the number in order of altitude of such tops as may be considered separate hills and their subsidiary tops respectively.

" Tops " and " Hills " were determined by the following rules:—

" Tops."—All elevations with a drop of 100 feet on all sides and elevations of sufficient topographical merit with a drop of between 100 feet and 50 feet on all sides.

" Hills."—Grouping of " tops " into " hills", except where in-applicable on topographical grounds, is on the basis that " tops " are not more than 17 units from the main top of the " hill " to which they belong, where a unit is either $\frac{1}{12}$ mile measured along the con-necting ridge or one 50-feet contour between the lower " top " and its connecting col.

While the rules as they stand rather lack mathematical precision, the actual result of their application is that, with but few exceptions, an 80-feet drop determines a " top " and the 17-unit rule a " hill".

Column 6—*Position.*—Four figure references have been used.

Column 7—*Summit.*—The information given in this column and in column 8 is intended to be of assistance in misty weather.   In this column are given, therefore, any distinguishing features by which the top may be recognised.   " No cairn " implies complete absence of any mark.   Figures thus, " 3×2", indicate the existence of a cairn 3 feet diameter by 2 feet height.   If the cairn is properly built with vertical sides it is described as " Stone man " and the size given as before.   Where the top has some distinguishing mark other than a cairn, this is described, *e.g.*, " Top at fence jct." or " Grassy flat 25 ft. diam."   A top not at the ordnance point is located from this by approximate distance and bearing.   " Top at fence " means either that the fence passes over the top, or that the summit is so flat that the top cannot be precisely located.   Tops $\frac{1}{8}$ mile or more from a fence are regarded as having no fence, but for distances from $\frac{1}{8}$ mile to $\frac{1}{4}$ mile particulars are given in column 8.

In column 7 " Top on N. side fence " implies that it is within 20 yards of the fence.   Such descriptions as " Top N. of fence " in column 7, or " Three fences meet S. of top " in column 8 imply that the distance is less than 100 yards.   Distances in excess of this are given to the nearest $\frac{1}{16}$ mile up to $\frac{1}{4}$ mile, and to the nearest $\frac{1}{8}$ mile thereafter.

Column 8—*Fences.*—Particulars are given of every main ridge fence and dike and of most junctions and subsidiary fences and dikes. Fence means a wire fence with wood or metal posts.   Dike means a dry stone wall.   Parenthetical qualifications of fences have the following meanings: " broken "—damaged condition but most of the material is present; " remains "—very dilapidated condition and most of the material is absent; " obliterated "—the original location can only be discerned by very close examination.   In order to follow this column a map showing county boundaries is necessary, and if it also shows parish boundaries, as do the 1-inch O.S. and $\frac{1}{2}$-inch Bartholomew maps, so much the better, but this is not essential, as all parish boundary fences and dikes are also located by a bearing or direction.

Table II

This Table gives the Scottish " hills " and " tops " only (including the two on the Union Boundary), arranged in order of height.

Columns 1 *and* 2 give the hill and top numbers, as given in columns 4 and 5 of Table I.

Column 3 gives the finally adjusted height only.

Column 4 gives the name, as given in column 1 of Table I.

Column 5 gives a reference to the Section number and the number of the top in that section so as to enable it to be readily found in Table I.

Table III

This is an alphabetical index to Table I and contains the name of every " hill", " top", and other elevation listed therein, and also includes names referred to in footnotes where these are likely to assist identification from tourist maps.

ABBREVIATIONS

Abbreviations.—b., by; B.M., Bench Mark; c., contour; C.B., County Boundary; Cr., Crown Tile; diam., diameter; fr., from; ft., feet; in., inches; jct., junction; m., mile; O.S., Ordnance Survey; P.B., Parish Boundary; Sta., Station; yds., yards.

TABLE I

THE 2000-FEET TOPS ARRANGED

NAME	HEIGHT	COUNTY and 1-in. O.S. Sheet No.		HILL No.	TOP No.

Section 1.—OCHIL HILLS.

NAME	HEIGHT	COUNTY and 1-in. O.S. Sheet No.		HILL No.	TOP No.
1. Blairdenon Hill	2,073	Perth and Clackmannan	55	72	107
2. Bencleuch[1]	2,363	Clackmannan . .	,,	24	35
3. Ben Ever . . . (2,000 c.)	2,010 ap.	do. . .	,,	...	127
4. The Law	2,094	do. . .	,,	...	100
5. Andrew Gannel Hill* . (2,150 c.)	2,196	do. . .	,,	...	72
6. King's Seat Hill . . (2,111)	2,125 ap.	do. . .	,,	64	89
7. Tarmangie Hill . . .	2,117	Perth and Clackmannan	,,	66	91
8. Whitewisp Hill . . .	2,110	Clackmannan . .	,,	...	94
9. Innerdownie	2,004	Perth . . .	,,	85	128

[1] Six-inch O.S. gives name as Ben Clach.

Section 2.—MOORFOOT HILLS.

NAME	HEIGHT	COUNTY and 1-in. O.S. Sheet No.		HILL No.	TOP No.
1. Jeffries Corse	2,040	Peebles . . .	62	78	118
2. Bowbeat Hill	2,050°	Midlothian and Peebles	,,	75	114
3. Blackhope Scar . . .	2,137°	Midlothian . .	,,	62	87
4. Whitehope Law . . .	2,038	Peebles . . .	,,	79	119
5. Windlestraw Law . . .	2,162	Peebles and Selkirk .	,,	58	81

Section 3.—TINTO HILLS.

NAME	HEIGHT	COUNTY and 1-in. O.S. Sheet No.		HILL No.	TOP No.
Tinto	2,335	Lanark . . .	68	27	41

Section 4.—CULTER HILLS.

NAME	HEIGHT	COUNTY and 1-in. O.S. Sheet No.		HILL No.	TOP No.
1. Chapelgill Hill	2,282	Peebles . . .	68	33	48
2. Cardon Hill	2,218	do. . . .	,,	...	65
3. Culter Fell	2,454	Lanark and Peebles .	,,	14	19
4. Heatherstone Law . . .	2,055	Lanark . . .	,,	74	113
5. Gathersnow Hill[1] . . .	2,262	Lanark and Peebles .	,,	41	56
6. Coomb Hill	2,096	Peebles . . .	,,	...	99
7. Hillshaw Head . . .	2,141	Lanark and Peebles .	,,	61	86
8. Coomb Dod	2,082	do. .	,,	...	105

[1] Named only Glenwhappen Rig on many maps.

TABLE I

According to Districts

Top No.	Position		Summit	Fences

Section 1.—OCHIL HILLS.

Top No.	Position		Summit	Fences
107	86	01	2 × 2 in N.W. fence angle .	Three fences meet; W. on P.B.; N.E. on C.B.; and S.E. slightly E. of C.B.
35	90	00	Two cairns 12 × 4 and indicator on S.W. side fence	
127	89	00	Grassy flat 5 ft. diam. $\frac{1}{16}$m. W. of fence	Fence on Bencleuch ridge to Ben Ever (jcts. N. to Ben Buck; and W. to Glenwinnel Burn);
100	91	99	6 × 3 on E. side fence	and to Andrew Gannel Hill* and stile on Right of Way at C.B. (jct. S. to The Law).
72	91	00	Top on S.E. side fence[2]	No fence.
89	93	99	3 × 1, $\frac{1}{8}$ m. N.W. fr. cairn; 30 × 7 at 2,111 point	
91	94	01	Top on N. side dike	
94	95	01	6 × 3	Dike on Tarmangie Hill on C.B., thence on ridge to Innerdownie (jct. fence S.E. on C.B., $\frac{1}{8}$ m. N.E. of Whitewisp, to Maiden's Well).
128	96	03	6 × 4 on N.W. side dike	

[2] The top of rocky outcrop $\frac{1}{16}$ m. S.E. fr. top is nearly the same height.

Section 2.—MOORFOOT HILLS.

Top No.	Position		Summit	Fences
118	28	49	Hollow grassy circle 6 ft. diam. containing stones S.W. of dike-fence angle	Dike to N.W.; fence to N.E. and 2,004 point (jct. S.E. to C.B.).
114	29	46	Top in N.W. fence angle	Four fences meet on Blackhope Scar; S.W. joining C.B. to Bowbeat Hill and Jeffries Corse (jct. W. at Leithen Water to Hog
87	31	48	6 × 4 of old fence posts on N. side fence jct.	Knowes); N.W. on P.B.; to E.; and S. joining C.B. thence to Whitehope Law (jcts.
119	33	44	Top at fence	N.E. at 1,965 point; E. on C.B. at 1,921 point; and E., $\frac{1}{4}$ m. N. fr. Whitehope Law).
81	37	43	Top at fence jct. . .	Four fences meet; to N.W.; N. and E. on C.B.; and S.W. to 2,147 point (jct. S.E. down Seathope Rig).

Section 3.—TINTO HILLS.

Top No.	Position		Summit	Fences
41	95	34	100 × 15 with cairns 12 × 4 and 9 × 3 on top at fence jct.	Two fences and two dikes meet; fences N. and N.E. on P.Bs.; dikes W. on P.B. to Howgate Mouth; and to S.E.

Section 4.—CULTER HILLS.

Top No.	Position		Summit	Fences
48	06	30	No cairn	No fence.
65	06	31	3 × 2 in N. fence angle	
19	05	29	5 × 3 on W. side fence	Fences on Cardon Hill down N. and N.E. ridges; and (remains) to angle in C.B. fence to Culter Fell and Glenwhappen Rig.
113	02	27	1 × $\frac{1}{4}$ on W. side fence . .	Three fences on P.Bs. meet S. of top; N. to Shankhoup Burn; S.E. to Hillshaw Burn only; and S.W. to Windgill Bank.
56	06	25	3 × 1 on N. side fence	
99	07	26	6 × 4 on E. side fence	
86	04	24	Top at fence	Fence on Gathersnow Hill on C.B. to Cultre Fell (jct. N.E. on P.B. to Coomb Hill); and to Hillshaw Head and Coomb Dod.
105	04	23	Grassy flat 20 ft. diam. at fence	

NAME	HEIGHT	COUNTY and 1-in. O.S. Sheet No.	HILL No.	TOP No.

Section 5.—MANOR HILLS.

NAME	HEIGHT	COUNTY and 1-in. O.S. Sheet No.		HILL No.	TOP No.
1. Birkscairn Hill	2,169	Peebles . . .	69	57	80
2. Dun Rig or Blackcleuch Head* . .	2,433	Peebles and Selkirk .	,,	16	22
3. Glenrath Heights (Middle Hill*) .	2,382	Peebles . . .	,,	21	29
4. Stob Law	2,218	do. . . .	,,	47	66
5. Black Law	2,285	Peebles and Selkirk .	,,	31	46
6. Blackhouse Heights (Black Cleuch Hill*)	2,214	do.	,,	...	69
7. Deer Law . . . (2,065)	2,067[1]	Selkirk . . .	,,	...	109
8. Greenside Law	2,110	Peebles and Selkirk .	,,	68	95
9. Pykestone Hill	2,414	Peebles . . .	,,	17	23
10. The Scrape	2,347	do. . . .	,,	...	39
11. Middle Hill*[2] . . . (2,400 c.)	2,340 ap.	do. . . .	,,	26	40
12. Taberon Law	2,088	do. . . .	,,	...	103
13. Drumelzier Law	2,191	do. . . .	,,	52	74
14. Dollar Law	2,680	do. . . .	,,	5	5
15. Fifescar Knowe	2,650	do. . . .	,,	...	8
16. Cramalt Craig	2,723	Peebles and Selkirk .	,,	3	3
17. Hunt Law	2,094	Peebles . . .	,,	...	101
18. Clockmore . . . (2,100)	2,105 ap.	Selkirk . . .	,,	...	96
19. Broad Law	2,754	Peebles and Selkirk .	,,	2	2
20. Talla Cleuch Head*[3] . . .	2,264	Peebles . . .	,,	39	54

[1] B.M. (from 6-inch O.S.) on surface rock.
[2] O.S. contours are very inaccurate here.   Grey Weather Law* (2,300 c.) 2,335, ¾ m. N. b. E. fr
Long Grain Knowe is nearly the same height.

Section 6.—MOFFAT HILLS.

NAME	HEIGHT	COUNTY and 1-in. O.S. Sheet No.		HILL No.	TOP No.
1. Erie Hill	2,259	Peebles . . .	69	42	57
2. Garelet Hill	2,231	do. . . .	,,	...	61
3. Laird's Cleuch Rig* (*Top above*) .	2,237	do. . . .	,,	...	60
4. Garelet Dod	2,263	do. . . .	,,	40	55
5. Molls Cleuch Dod	2,571	do. . . .	,,	11	14
6. Carlavin Hill	2,383	do. . . .	,,	...	28
7. Lochcraig Head	2,625	Peebles and Selkirk .	,,	8	11
8. Nickies Knowe	2,492	do.	,,	...	17
9. White Coomb	2,695	Dumfries . . .	,,	4	4

TOP No.	POSITION		SUMMIT	FENCES

Section 5.—MANOR HILLS.

TOP No.	POSITION		SUMMIT	FENCES
				C.B. fence is continuous Dun Rig to Lochcraig Head (*Section* 6).
80	27	33	9 × 5 in W. fence angle .	Three fences meet; to N.W.; to N.E.; and S.W. on P.B. to Dun Rig.
22	25	31	Top at fence jct. . . .	Three fences meet on C.B. and P.B.
29	24	32	3 × 1	No fence.
66	23	33	No cairn	do.
46	21	27	Top at fence jct. . .	Three fences meet; S. to Deer Law; and on C.B. (jct. E. near 2,283 point).
69	22	29	Top at fence .	Fence on C.B. (remains only for 1¼ m. N.E.).
109	22	25	Standing stone 3 ft. 6 in. height ⅟₁₆ m. W. of fence .	Fence N. to Black Law; and E. down ridge.
95	19	25	Top N.W. of fence .	Fence on C.B.
23	17	31	6 × 2 some yds. S.E. . .	No fence.
39	17	32	2 × 1 with post on grassy flat 15 ft. diam. on S.E. side fence jct.	Two fences meet; N.W. to Scawd Law; and N.E. (broken) on P.B. (jct. E. down ridge).
40	16	29	No cairn . . .	No fence.
103	14	29	do.	do.
74	14	31	6 × 2	do.
5	17	27	6 × 3 on grassy patch 20 ft. diam. on W. side dike	Two dikes and fence meet N. of Dollar Law; fence N.W. on P.B. ending at Long Grain Knowe; dikes E. down ridge; and S. on P.B. to C.B. fence angle.
8	17	27	Top at dike	
3	17	25	6 × 4 on S.E. side fence . .	Three fences meet; W. to Hunt Law; and on C.B.
101	15	26	Top on S.W. side fence .	Fence on ridge S.E. to Cramalt Craig.
96	18	22	Top ⅟₁₆ m. W. fr. 2,100 point	No fence.
2	14	23	4 × 3 on W. side fence . .	Fence on C.B. Dike fr. Polmood Burn to Wylies Burn crosses half-way to 2,723 point (4 × 3 on S. side fence).
54	13	21	Top at fence . . .	Fence on ridge to Cairn Law on C.B. fence.

³ One-inch O.S. gives name Muckle Side only.

Section 6.—MOFFAT HILLS.

TOP No.	POSITION		SUMMIT	FENCES
				C.B. dike or fence is continuous Lochcraig Head to Hart Fell.
57	12	18	3 × 1 on N. side dike . .	Dike W. down ridge; and E. to main N. to S. dike.
61	12	20	Two posts N.E. of dike .	Fence N.W. down ridge; dike S.E. to Laird's Cleuch Rig.*
60	12	19	Top W. of dike . .	Dike N. to Garelet Hill; and S. to Din Law.
55	12	17	No cairn	Dike ⅜ m. E. fr. top.
14	15	18	Top at dike	Dike runs Gameshope Burn (fence at first), Carlavin Hill, Molls Cleuch Dod, Firthybrig Head (joining C.B. dike).
28	14	19	do.	
11	16	17	Two turf circles, one with post, one with rain gauge, on W. side fence	Fence on C.B. (jct. to N.E. at Talla East Side) joining Dumfries C.B. dike.
17	16	19	Top at fence . . .	Fence on C.B.
4	16	15	3 × 1 on grassy flat 20 ft. diam. ⅟₁₆ m. S. of dike	Dike W. to C.B. dike at Firthhope Rig; and E. down ridge.

Name	Height	County and 1-in. O.S. Sheet No.	Hill No.	Top No.
Section 6.—MOFFAT HILLS.				
10. Great Hill	2,540	Peebles . . . 69	...	15
11. Firthhope Rig	2,627	Peebles and Dumfries ,,	...	10
12. Carrifran Gans	2,452	Dumfries . . . ,,	...	20
13. Cape Law	2,364	Peebles . . . ,,	23	34
14. Din Law	2,182	do. . . . ,,	...	76
15. Under Saddle Yoke* . (2,400 c.)	2,445 ap.	Dumfries . . . ,,	15	21
16. Saddle Yoke	2,412	do. . . . ,,	...	24
17. Whitehope Heights* . . (2,050 c.)	2,090 ap.	Peebles and Dumfries 68	70	102
18. Hart Fell	2,651	do. . 69	7	7
19. Swatte Fell . . . (2,388)	2,390	Dumfries . . . ,,	20	27
20. Falcon Craig* (*Top above*) . . .	2,373	do. . . . ,,	...	32
21. Nether Coomb Craig (*Top above*) .	2,373	do. . . . ,,	...	33
Section 7.—ETTRICK HILLS.				
1. Herman Law	2,014°	Dumfries and Selkirk . 69	84	126
2. Andrewhinney Hill	2,220	do. . ,,	46	64
3. Trowgrain Middle	2,058°	Dumfries . . . ,,	...	112
4. Bell Craig	2,046	Dumfries and Selkirk . ,,	76	116
5. Mid Rig* . . (2,000 c.)	2,018[1]	do. . ,,	...	125
6. Bodesbeck Law	2,173	Dumfries . . . ,,	56	79
7. Capel Fell	2,223	Dumfries and Selkirk . ,,	45	63
8. Smidhope Hill* . (2,100 c.)	2,111	do. . ,,	...	93
9. White Shank	2,035°	do. . ,,	...	120
10. Ettrick Pen	2,270	do. . ,,	36	51
11. Wind Fell	2,180	do. . ,,	54	77
12. Hopetoun Craig	2,075	do. . ,,	...	106
13. Loch Fell (East Knowe*) . . .	2,256	Dumfries . . . ,,	43	59
14. Loch Fell (West Knowe*) . (2,150 c.)	2,196[2]	do. . ,,	...	73
15. Croft Head	2,085	do. . ,,	71	104

[1] Six-inch O.S. gives B.M. 2018·1.
[2] A second point to N. and nearer the dike is nearly the same height.

Top No.	Position		Summit	Fences

Section 6.—MOFFAT HILLS.

Top No.	Position		Summit	Fences
15	14	16	No cairn	No fence.
10	15	15	Top at dike . .	Dike on C.B. (jct. N. fr. top, E. to White Coomb) (fence across Rotten Bottom).
20	15	13	2×1	No fence.
34	13	15	Top S.W. of dike .	Dike N.W. to Din Law; and S.E. to C.B. fence-dike angle.
76	12	15	Top 1/16 m. S.W. of dike .	Dike N. to Laird's Cleuch Rig,* and S.E. to Cape Law.
21	14	12	No cairn	No fence.
24	14	12	6×3 some yds. S.W. . .	do.
102	09	13	No cairn	do.
7	11	13	15×4, crescent shaped, on S.W. side fence angle	Fence on C.B.N. down ridge; and N.E. to Cape Law ridge dike. Fence (obliterated) S. to Auchencat Burn col.
27	11	11	Top at dike, 1/2 m. N.E. fr. 2,388 point[1]	Dike on Swatte Fell N.E. to Auchencat Burn col thence down burn; and S.W. down ridge.
32	12	12	Top W. of dike	
33	13	11	No cairn	No fence.

[1] A cairn 2×1, 1/4 m. E. fr. top, is nearly the same height.

Section 7.—ETTRICK HILLS.

Top No.	Position		Summit	Fences
				C.B. fence (or dike) is continuous Herman Law to Ettrick Pen.
126	21	15	Top at fence jct.	
64	19	13	10×2 with three posts on N. side fence	Three fences meet on Herman Law; W. on C.B.; E. down face; and S. on C.B.
112	20	14	Top 1/16 m. N.W. of fence and stone man 3 ft. square by 5 ft. height on E. side fence	
116	18	12	Top at fence jct. . . .	Three fences meet; two on C.B.; and (broken) S.E. down ridge.
125	18	12	Top at fence	
79	16	10	Grassy flat 10 ft. diam. with stones in central hole W. of dike[2]	At 1,991 point meet; fence on C.B. fr. Mid Rig*; dike fr. S.E.; and dike on C.B. fr. Bodesbeck Law.
63	16	07	Top at fence (broken)	Fence (broken) on C.B. for 1/2 m. on Capel Fell thence dike on C.B. to Bodesbeck Law (jct. N.W. down Sailfoot Linn); and fence on C.B. to Wind Fell (jct. S.W. down Capel Fell ridge).
93	16	07	Top at dike[3]	
120	16	08	Top N.E. of dike	
51	19	07	5×4 in S.E. fence angle	Three fences meet on Ettrick Pen; N.W. on C.B.; E. down ridge; and S.E. on C.B. to Wind Fell.
77	17	06	Top at fence	
106	18	06	5×2 on E. side fence	
59	17	04	Top at fence jct.	Four fences on P.B.s meet; N. to C.B. fence at Wind Fell (jct. E. to Cauld Law); S. to Dun Moss; S.W. to Cowan Fell; and (remains) N.W. to West Knowe* and Croft Head.
73	16	05	Top at fence (remains)	
104	15	05	Top at fence jct. . . .	Three fences meet; to N.W.; S. on P.B.; and (broken) S.E. on P.B. to Loch Fell.

[3] Two other points to N. and S. are nearly the same height.
[4] Six-inch O.S. gives B.M. 2196·3.

Name		Height	County and 1-in. O.S. Sheet No.		Hill No.	Top No.

Section 8.—LOWTHER HILLS.

1. Lousie Wood Law		2,028	Lanark . . . 68		81	122
2. Dun Law		2,216	do. . . . ,,		48	67
3. Green Lowther		2,403	do. . . . ,,		19	26
4. Lowther Hill		2,377	Dumfries and Lanark ,,		22	31
5. Comb Head . .	(2,000 c.)	2,060 ap.	do. . ,,		...	111
6. East Mount Lowther . .		2,068	Dumfries . . . ,,		73	108
Comb Law . . .	(2,107)	2,120 ap.	Lanark . . . ,,		65	90
8. Ballencleuch Law . . .		2,267	do. . . . ,,		38	53
9. Rodger Law		2,257	do. . . . ,,		...	58
10. Scaw'd Law . .	(2,166)	2,180[1]	Dumfries and Lanark ,,		55	78
11. Glenleith Fell		2,003°	Dumfries . . . ,,		...	129
12. Wedder Law . .	(2,200 c.)	2,206[2]	Dumfries and Lanark ,,		51	71
13. Gana Hill		2,190°	do. . ,,		53	75
14. Earncraig Hill		2,000	do. . ,,		86	132
15. Queensberry		2,285	Dumfries . . . ,,		32	47

[1] Six-inch O.S. gives nearby B.M. 2179·6.

Section 9.—CARSPHAIRN HILLS.

1. Blackcraig Hill . . .		2,298	Ayr . . . 67		29	44
2. Blacklorg		2,231	Ayr and Dumfries . ,,		44	62
3. Meikledodd Hill . . (2,100 c.)		2,100 ap.	Kirkcudbright . . ,,		...	97
4. Alhang . . . (2,100 c.)		2,100 ap.	Ayr and Kirkcudbright ,,		69	98
5. Alwhat		2,063	do. ,,		...	110
6. Windy Standard . . (2,287)		2,288	Kirkcudbright . . ,,		30	45
7. Dugland . . . (2,000 c.)		2,000[1]	do. . . ,,		...	133
8. Moorbrock Hill . . .		2,136°	do. . . ,,		63	88
9. Cairnsmore of Carsphairn . .		2,612°	do. . . ,,		9	12
10. Beninner		2,328°	do. . . ,,		...	43

[1] Six-inch O.S. gives very small 2,000-ft. contour.

Section 10.—GALLOWAY HILLS

1. Coran of Portmark . . .		2,042°	Kirkcudbright . . 73		77	117
2. Bow . . . (2,000 c.)		2,002 ap.	do. . . ,,		...	130
3. Meaul		2,280°	do. . . ,,		35	50
4. Cairnsgarroch		2,155°	do. . . ,,		59	83
5. Corserine		2,668	do. . . ,,		6	6
6. Carlin's Cairn . . (2,650 c.)		2,650	do. . . ,,		...	9
7. Milldown . . (2,400 c.)		2,410 ap.	do. . . ,,		18	25

Top No.	Position		Summit	Fences

Section 8.—LOWTHER HILLS.

Top No.	Position		Summit	Fences
122	93	15	6 × 3 N.W. of fence-dike jct.	Three fences meet on Lousie Wood Law; fences and dikes down N.E. and W. ridges;
67	91	13	Top at fence	fence S.W. to Dun Law and Peden Head* (¾ m. N.E. b. E. fr. Green Lowther) thence S.E. to Riccart Law Rig.
26	90	12	6 × 3	No fence.
31	89	10	6 × 4	do.
111	89	09	No cairn	do.
108	87	10	Grassy flat 25 ft. diam. .	do.
90	94	07	Top on S.E. side fence ⅛ m. S. fr. 2,107 point	Two dikes and fence meet N. of top; dikes N.W. and N.E. down ridges; fence (broken) S.W. to Ballencleuch Law.
53	93	05	Top at fence . . .	Fence (broken) N.E. to Comb Law; and S.W. to C.B. dike on Scaw'd Law.
58	94	05	No cairn	No fence.
78	92	03	Top at dike ¼ m. N. fr. 2,166 point	Dike on C.B.
129	92	02	Top E. of fence . . .	Fence on P.B. to C.B. dike on Scaw'd Law at 2,166 point.
71	93	02	Top at fence (remains) ⅛ m. N. fr. 2,185 point	Fence (remains) on C.B. N.W. to Scaw'd Law (becomes dike in col); and S. to Berry Grain only.
75	95	01	6 × 4 some yds. N.E. .	No fence.
132	97	01	Top at dike . .	Two fences and dike meet N.E. of top; dike S.W. on C.B. to col only; fences N. on C.B.; and N.E. on P.B. to shoulder of Queensberry.
47	99	99	20 × 8	Fence on P.B. ¼ m. N.E. fr. top.

[2] Six-inch O.S. gives nearby B.M. 2206·2.

Section 9.—CARSPHAIRN HILLS.

Top No.	Position		Summit	Fences
44	64	06	12 × 6 with two posts . .	Fence (obliterated) N. to S.
62	65	04	Top at dike-fence jct. . .	Dike to Cannock Hill; fence on C.B. to Meikledodd Hill.
97	66	03	Top N.E. of fence . .	Fence N.W. to C.B. fence; and S. down ridge.
98	64	01	3 × 1, 1/16 m. S.E. of fence .	Fence N.W. of C.B. to Alwhat; and on C.B. down N.W. ridge to col.
110	64	02	Top at fence jct. . .	Three fences meet; (remains) on C.B. to Meikledodd Hill; S.E. on P.B. to Ewe Hill; and N.W. of C.B. to Alhang.
45	62	01	3 × 2	No fence.
133	60	00	3 × 1	do.
88	61	98	No cairn	do.
12	59	98	20 × 8 at dike end . .	Dike S.W. to Gold Wells.
43	60	97	4 × 3	No fence.

Section 10.—GALLOWAY HILLS.

Top No.	Position		Summit	Fences
117	50	93	9 × 2	No fence.
130	50	92	2 × 2[1]	do.
50	50	91	4 × 3 S.E. of dike-fence jct. .	Fence (remains) N. to dike down Garryhorn Burn; and dike E. to Cairnsgarroch.
83	51	91	Top on S. side dike .	Dike W. to Meaul; and N.E. down ridge.
6	49	87	3 × 2	No fence.
9	49	88	40 × 6 with cairn 6 × 6 on top	do.
25	51	84	Top at dike . . .	Dike N.W. to cross dike in Milldown-Millfire col.; and S.E. to Meikle Millyea.

[1] The top is the northmost of the three 2,000-ft. contours shown on the 1-inch O.S.

NAME		HEIGHT	COUNTY and 1-in. O.S. Sheet No.	HILL No.	TOP No.

Section 10.—GALLOWAY HILLS—*Continued*

NAME		HEIGHT	COUNTY and 1-in. O.S. Sheet No.	HILL No.	TOP No.
8. Millfire		2,350	Kirkcudbright . . 73	...	37
9. Meikle Millyea . . (2,450 c.)		2,455	do. . ,,	13	18
10. Mullwharcher		2,270°	Ayr . . . . ,,	37	52
11. Dungeon Hill . . . (2,000 c.)		2,020 ap.	Kirkcudbright . . ,,	83	124
12. Craignaw		2,115°	do. . ,,	67	92
13. Shalloch on Minnoch . (2,520)		2,528	Ayr . . . . ,,	12	16
14. do. (N. Top) .		2,162	do. . . . . ,	...	82
15. Tarfessock		2,282°	do. . . . . ,,	34	49
16. do. (S. Top) . (2,000 c.)		2,050 ap.	do. . . . . ,,	...	115
17. Kirriereoch Hill . . (2,565)		2,575 ap.	Kirkcudbright . . ,,	10	13
18. Merrick		2,764°	do. . . ,,	1	1
19. Benyellary		2,360°	do. . . ,,	...	36
20. Lamachan Hill . . (2,350 c.)		2,350²	do. . . ,,	25	38
21. Larg Hill		2,216°	do. . . ,,	49	68
22. Curleywee		2,212°	do. . . ,,	50	70
23. Millfore . . . . (2,150 c.)		2,151⁴	do. . . ,,	60	85
24. Cairnsmore of Fleet . . (2,329)		2,331	do. . . ,,	28	42
25. Meikle Mulltaggart . . (2,000 c.)		2,000 ap.	do. . . ,,	...	131
26. Knee of Cairnsmore . . (2,152)		2,154⁶	do. . . ,,	...	84

¹ The westmost of two small cairns beside the C.B. dike may be the 2,565 point.
² Six-inch O.S. gives very small 2,350-ft. contour.
³ Cairn 2×2 on S.E. side dike-fence jct. Six-inch O.S. shows top ⅛ m. N. fr. dike-fence jct., but there is no cairn and the summit plateau is practically level.

Section 11.—ROXBURGH HILLS.

NAME		HEIGHT	COUNTY and 1-in. O.S. Sheet No.	HILL No.	TOP No.
Cauldcleuch Head . . . (2,000 c.)		2,028	Roxburgh . . . 69	82	123

Section 12.—CHEVIOT HILLS.
SCOTLAND AND ENGLAND

NAME		HEIGHT	COUNTY and 1-in. O.S. Sheet No.	HILL No.	TOP No.
1. Windy Gyle		2,034	Roxburgh & Northumberland 70	80	121
2. Auchope Cairn		2,382¹	do. ,,	...	30

ENGLAND

NAME		HEIGHT	COUNTY and 1-in. O.S. Sheet No.	HILL No.	TOP No.
3. The Cheviot		2,676	Northumberland . 71	...	...
4. Hedgehope Hill		2,348	do. . ,,	...	...
5. Comb Fell . . . (2,132)		2,160 ap.	do. . ,,	...	...
6. Bloodybush Edge		2,001	do. . ,,	...	...
7. Cushat Law		2,020	do. . ,,	...	...

¹ The highest point on the Union Boundary is (2,419) 2,422.

Top No.	Position		Summit	Fences

Section 10.—GALLOWAY HILLS—*Continued.*

Top No.	Pos.		Summit	Fences
37	50	84	3 × 3	No fence.
18	51	82	4 × 4 W. of dike ¼ m. S.S.W. fr. 2,446 point	Dike to Milldown; and S. down ridge.
52	45	86	2 × 1 with vertical stone .	No fence.
124	46	85	Stone man 2 × 3 . . .	do.
92	45	83	4 × 4	do.
16	40	90	Top ¼ m. S.E. b. E. fr. cairn 15 × 5 at 2,520 point	do.
82	40	92	Hole 4 ft. diam. with stones .	do.
49	40	89	3 × 3	do.
115	41	88	2 × 1	do.
13	41	87	Top 1/16 m. S. of dike and 1/16 m. S.E. fr. 2,565 point[1]	Dike on C.B.
1	42	85	15 × 7	No fence.
36	41	83	6 × 3 E. of dike . . .	Dike to W. shoulder of Merrick; and S.W. down ridge.
38	43	77	Top at dike-fence jct. or ⅛ m. N.[3]	Fence and two dikes meet; fence N.E. to cross dike in Nick of Curleywee; dikes down W. face; and to Larg Hill (jct. W. in col).
68	42	75	2 × ½ N.W. of dike jct. . .	Three dikes meet; N.E. to Lamachan Hill; S. and S.W. down ridges.
70	45	76	6 × 3	No fence.
85	47	75	6 × 2[5]	do.
42	50	67	9 × 7 Stone hut and flat cairn E. fr. top	do.
131	51	67	No cairn	do.
84	51	65	9 × 7	do.

[4] Six-inch O.S. gives nearby Cr. 2151·0.
[5] Similar cairn farther to N.E.
[6] Six-inch O.S. gives nearby Cr. 2154·7.

Section 11.—ROXBURGH HILLS.

123	45	00	Top at right-angle bend in fence above S. ridge ¼ m. W.S.W. fr. 1,996 point	Fence down E. ridge on P.B.; and down S. ridge.

Section 12.—CHEVIOT HILLS.

SCOTLAND AND ENGLAND

121	85	15	50 × 7 with cairns 12 × 7 and 6 × 4 on top	No fence.
30	89	19	4 × 3	do.

ENGLAND

...	90	20	Top marked by wood posts and broken bottles	No fence.
...	94	19	40 × 5 with cairn 12 × 5 on top at fence jct.	Three fences meet; to Comb Fell; to E.; and to S.E.
...	91	18	Top at fence ⅜ m. E. b. N. fr. 2,132 point	Fence to W.; and to Hedgehope Hill.
...	90	14	Top at end of fence . .	Fence to W.
...	92	13	30 × 6 some yds. N. . .	No fence.

NAME		HEIGHT	COUNTY and 1-in. 7th. O.S. Sheet No.		

Section 13.—APPENDIX.

The following points are not " tops", but each is enclosed by an isolated 2,000-ft. contour.

NAME		HEIGHT	COUNTY	and 1-in. 7th. O.S. Sheet No.	
1. Greenforet Hill*		2,020	Perth . . .	55	Section 1
2. Jeffries Corse (N. Top) . . .		2,004	Midlothian and Peebles	62	,, 2
3. Birks Hill . . . (2,030)		2,045 ap.	Peebles . . .	69	,, 5
4. White Cleuch Hill		2,004	Peebles and Selkirk .	,,	,, 5
5. Conscleuch Head		2,039	Selkirk . . .	,,	,, 5
6. Greenside Law (S. Top) . . .		2,004	do. . . .	,,	,, 5
7. Shielhope Head or Water Head . .		2,011	Peebles and Selkirk .	,,	,, 5
8. Ellers Cleuch Rig		2,005	Peebles . . .	,,	,, 6
9. Whitehope Knowe*[1] . . .		2,012	Peebles and Dumfries	68	,, 6
10. Comb Head (E. Top) . (2,000 c.)		2,039[2]	Dumfries and Lanark	,,	,, 8
11. Trostan Hill . . . (2,000 c.)		2,035 ap.	Kirkcudbright . .	67	,, 9
12. Keoch Rig . . . (2,000 c.)		2,020 ap.	do. .	,,	,, 9
13. Bow (M. Top) . . . (2,000 c.)		2,000 ap.	do. . .	73	,, 10
14. Bow (S. Top) . . . (2,000 c.)		2,001 ap.	do. . .	,,	,, 10
15. Millfore (S. Top) . . (2,000 c.)		2,025 ap.	do. . .	,,	,, 10

[1] One-inch O.S. gives name Barry Grain Rig only.

POSITION	SUMMIT	FENCES

Section 13.—APPENDIX.

The following points are not " tops," but each is enclosed by an isolated 2,000-ft. contcur.

POSITION		SUMMIT	FENCES
86	01	Top S.W. of fence . .	Fence on P.B. to N.W.; and to Blairdenon Hill.
28	49	Top at fence . . .	Fence down N. ridge; and to Jeffries Corse.
28	33	Top $\frac{1}{8}$ m. S.W. fr. cairn 9×3 at 2,030 point	No fence.
22	29	Top at fence (remains) .	Fence (remains) on C.B. to Dun Rig; and to Blackhouse Heights.
22	26	Top at fence . . .	Fence to Black Law; and to Deer Law.
19	25	No cairn	No fence.
19	25	Top at fence . . .	Fence on C.B. to Greenside Law; and to Cramalt Craig.
12	16	Top W. of dike . . .	Dike N. to Garelet Dod; and S. to Din Law.
09	14	No cairn	No fence.
90	09	do.	do.
61	01	do.	do.
61	00	Top $\frac{1}{16}$ m. S.E. of fence .	Fence S.W. to Bow Burn; and N.E. to Old Mines.
50	92	No cairn	No fence.
50	92	5×3 some yds. W. . .	do.
47	75	5×4	do.

[2] Six-inch O.S. gives nearby B.M. 2039·1.

TABLE II

The 2000-Feet Tops Arranged in

Order of Altitude

Hill No.	Top No.	Height	Name	Ref. to Table I.
1	1	2,764	Merrick	10-18
2	2	2,754	Broad Law	5-19
3	3	2,723	Cramalt Craig	5-16
4	4	2,695	White Coomb	6-9
5	5	2,680	Dollar Law	5-14
6	6	2,668	Corserine	10-5
7	7	2,651	Hart Fell	6-18
...	8	2,650	Fifescar Knowe	5-15
...	9	2,650	Carlin's Cairn	10-6
...	10	2,627	Firthhope Rig	6-11
8	11	2,625	Lochcraig Head	6-7
9	12	2,612	Cairnsmore of Carsphairn	9-9
10	13	2,575 ap.	Kirriereoch Hill	10-17
11	14	2,571	Molls Cleuch Dod	6-5
...	15	2,540	Great Hill	6-10
12	16	2,528	Shalloch on Minnoch	10-13
...	17	2,492	Nickies Knowe	6-8
13	18	2,455	Meikle Millyea	10-9
14	19	2,454	Culter Fell	4-3
...	20	2,452	Carrifran Gans	6-12
15	21	2,445 ap.	Under Saddle Yoke*	6-15
16	22	2,433	Dun Rig or Blackcleuch Head*	5-2
17	23	2,414	Pykestone Hill	5-9
...	24	2,412	Saddle Yoke	6-16
18	25	2,410 ap.	Milldown	10-7
19	26	2,403	Green Lowther	8-3
20	27	2,390	Swatte Fell	6-19
...	28	2,383	Carlavin Hill	6-6
21	29	2,382	Glenrath Heights (Middle Hill*)	5-3
...	30	2,382	Auchope Cairn	12-2
22	31	2,377	Lowther Hill	8-4
...	32	2,373	Falcon Craig* (*Top above*)	6-20
...	33	2,373	Nether Coomb Craig (*Top above*)	6-21
23	34	2,364	Cape Law	6-13
24	35	2,363	Bencleuch	1-2
...	36	2,360	Benyellary	10-19
...	37	2,350	Millfire	10-8
25	38	2,350	Lamachan Hill	10-20
...	39	2,347	The Scrape	5-10
26	40	2,340 ap.	Middle Hill*	5-11
27	41	2,335	Tinto	3
28	42	2,331	Cairnsmore of Fleet	10-24
...	43	2,328	Beninner	9-10
29	44	2,298	Blackcraig Hill	9-1
30	45	2,288	Windy Standard	9-6
31	46	2,285	Black Law	5-5
32	47	2,285	Queensberry	8-15
33	48	2,282	Chapelgill Hill	4-1
34	49	2,282	Tarfessock	10-15
35	50	2,280	Meaul	10-3
36	51	2,270	Ettrick Pen	7-10
37	52	2,270	Mullwharcher	10-10
38	53	2,267	Ballencleuch Law	8-8
39	54	2,264	Talla Cleuch Head*	5-20
40	55	2,263	Garelet Dod	6-4
41	56	2,262	Gathersnow Hill	4-5
42	57	2,259	Erie Hill	6-1
...	58	2,257	Rodger Law	8-9

TABLE II—*Continued.*

Hill No.	Top No.	Height	Name	Ref. to Table I.
43	59	2,256	Loch Fell (East Knowe*)	7-13
...	60	2,237	Laird's Cleuch Rig* (*Top above*)	6-3
...	61	2,231	Garelet Hill	6-2
44	62	2,231	Blacklorg	9-2
45	63	2,223	Capel Fell	7-7
46	64	2,220	Andrewhinney Hill	7-2
...	65	2,218	Cardon Hill	4-2
47	66	2,218	Stob Law	5-4
48	67	2,216	Dun Law	8-2
49	68	2,216	Larg Hill	10-21
...	69	2,214	Blackhouse Heights (Black Cleuch Hill*)	5-6
50	70	2,212	Curleywee	10-22
51	71	2,206	Wedder Law	8-12
...	72	2,196	Andrew Gannel Hill*	1-5
...	73	2,196	Loch Fell (West Knowe*)	7-14
52	74	2,191	Drumelzier Law	5-13
53	75	2,190	Gana Hill	8-13
...	76	2,182	Din Law	6-14
54	77	2,180	Wind Fell	7-11
55	78	2,180	Scaw'd Law	8-10
56	79	2,173	Bodesbeck Law	7-6
57	80	2,169	Birkscairn Hill	5-1
58	81	2,162	Windlestraw Law	2-5
...	82	2,162	Shalloch on Minnoch (N. top)	10-14
59	83	2,155	Cairnsgarroch	10-4
...	84	2,154	Knee of Cairnsmore	10-26
60	85	2,151	Millfore	10-23
61	86	2,141	Hillshaw Head	4-7
62	87	2,137	Blackhope Scar	2-3
63	88	2,136	Moorbrock Hill	9-8
64	89	2,125 ap.	King's Seat Hill	1-6
65	90	2,120 ap.	Comb Law	8-7
66	91	2,117	Tarmangie Hill	1-7
67	92	2,115	Craignaw	10-12
...	93	2,111	Smidhope Hill*	7-8
...	94	2,110	Whitewisp Hill	1-8
68	95	2,110	Greenside Law	5-8
...	96	2,105 ap.	Clockmore	5-18
...	97	2,100 ap.	Meikledodd Hill	9-3
69	98	2,100 ap.	Alhang	9-4
...	99	2,096	Coomb Hill	4-6
...	100	2,094	The Law	1-4
...	101	2,094	Hunt Law	5-17
70	102	2,090 ap.	Whitehope Heights*	6-17
...	103	2,088	Taberon Law	5-12
71	104	2,085	Croft Head	7-15
...	105	2,082	Coomb Dod	4-8
...	106	2,075	Hopetoun Craig	7-12
72	107	2,073	Blairdenon Hill	1-1
73	108	2,068	East Mount Lowther	8-6
...	109	2,067	Deer Law	5-7
...	110	2,063	Alwhat	9-5
...	111	2,060 ap.	Comb Head	8-5
...	112	2,058	Trowgrain Middle	7-3
74	113	2,055	Heatherstane Law	4-4

TABLE II—*Continued.*

Hill No.	Top No.	Height	Name	Ref. to Table I.
75	114	2,050	Bowbeat Hill	2-2
...	115	2,050 ap.	Tarfessock (S. top)	10-16
76	116	2,046	Bell Craig	7-4
77	117	2,042	Coran of Portmark	10-1
78	118	2,040	Jeffries Corse	2-1
79	119	2,038	Whitehope Law	2-4
...	120	2,035	White Shank	7-9
80	121	2,034	Windy Gyle	12-1
81	122	2,028	Lousie Wood Law	8-1
82	123	2,028	Cauldcleuch Head	11
83	124	2,020 ap.	Dungeon Hill	10-1
...	125	2,018	Mid Rig*	7-5
84	126	2,014	Herman Law	7-1
...	127	2,010 ap.	Ben Ever	1-3
85	128	2,004	Innerdownie	1-9
...	129	2,003	Glenleith Fell	8-11
...	130	2,002 ap.	Bow	10-2
...	131	2,000 ap.	Meikle Mulltaggart	10-25
86	132	2,000	Earncraig Hill	8-14
...	133	2,000	Dugland	9-7

TABLE III

ALPHABETICAL INDEX TO TABLE I

TABLE III—*Continued.*

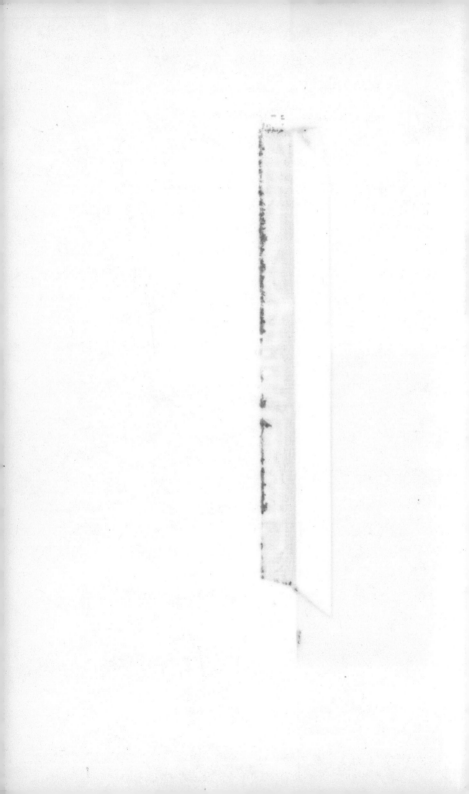